Henry Ward Beecher

The crown of life

Henry Ward Beecher

The crown of life

ISBN/EAN: 9783337273163

Printed in Europe, USA, Canada, Australia, Japan

Cover: Foto ©Suzi / pixelio.de

More available books at **www.hansebooks.com**

THE CROWN OF LIFE

FROM THE WRITINGS OF

HENRY WARD BEECHER

EDITED BY

MARY STORRS HAYNES

WITH INTRODUCTION BY

ROSSITER W RAYMOND

BOSTON
D. LOTHROP COMPANY
WASHINGTON STREET OPPOSITE BROMFIELD

INTRODUCTION.

It is both delightful and difficult to describe the characteristics of Henry Ward Beecher. We who knew him love to recall his words and ways; and each of us, like a lover sketching the features of the absent beloved, makes picture after picture, bearing for us some trait of likeness, yet not complete and satisfactory, even for us — how much less, then, for those who would seek by such means to gain acquaintance with a stranger, not merely to be reminded of a familiar friend!

Additional tributes of love and admiration to Mr. Beecher's memory are not needed. On the other hand, the time has not come for a critical estimate of his influence upon the political and religious history of his times, and the permanent value of his contributions to both. It is still too early even to pronounce upon the results of that work which was to him the noblest and dearest of all: the establishment of Plymouth Church, and its spiritual education through his views of doctrine and duty. As the first pastor of that church, he drew to it those who liked the minister, and were willing to receive instruction from him. And for forty years he impressed his teachings, not only upon adults trained already in other churches, but upon a new generation, of which, from its childhood, he was the guide. That generation, now in its prime, is the fruit and test of his labors. If it has been fed on oratory, "personal magnetism", sentimentalism and weakening heresy, under the taking title of "the Gospel of Love", its failure now will be the failure of Mr. Beecher's *system*, though it will not disprove his own sincerity and devotion in the propagation of error. But if, on the contrary, the Plymouth Church that gathered and grew up around him continues after he is gone a true church of Christ, united, fervent, active, and victoriously aggressive in the work for which he trained it, the candid observer will confess that a seal of final authority has been set upon the truth he taught and the motives he inspired.

This crucial test is in progress. It is only fair to say that all friendly fears and hostile prophecies have been disappointed hitherto. The church that was supposed to be a heterogeneous mass, held together only by the attraction of one personality, and certain either to disintegrate in indifference or be rent asunder by internal repulsions as soon as this harmonizing element should be withdrawn, has, on the contrary, gathering new inspiration from sorrow, presented thus far a spectacle of harmony, zeal and organized activity, confounding all the prophets of disaster. Fluent predictions have given place to fluent explanations, equally superficial. Time will show whether the true, deep explanation be not the Divine truth expounded by Mr. Beecher, applied by him as a motive to every human life, and illustrated in his own. But this momentous verdict cannot be rendered yet. Faith may anticipate it; history only can record it.

If it be, then, too late for eulogy and too early for history, what shall be written now? It seems to me that this is the time for recording such facts and views about Mr. Beecher as may be of use hereafter in forming that conception of him and his work which will be the possession of humanity after all his contemporaries shall have passed away—a conception which no single statement can now express, but to which every trustworthy contribution will be of value.

Such a contribution I am enabled to make from a personal acquaintance beginning in my boyhood, and especially from a closer companionship, in certain departments of study, during the last twenty years of Mr. Beecher's life. To be more precise, we read and discussed together certain books and theories, particularly such as bore upon the relations of Christianity to modern science and criticism. I was enabled by my professional education to assist him in his examination of various hypotheses, and his estimation of the drift of scientific thought, although, apart from any such suggestions, he was himself a deep, close student, and in certain lines of science (such as botany) greatly my superior. On the other hand, I need not say, any slight service which he may have received in this way was immeasurably overpaid with such assistance as no mere study could supply. To pursue an investigation in such company was like journeying with some strong angel, who would go afoot for awhile, exploring like other people — would even, perhaps, indulgently let me take the lead, but where the labyrinth had overgrown the path, or some abyss or cliff seemed to cut it off, would open mighty wings of power and lift me high in air, giving me, in lieu of petty guidance, one broad survey, that showed the whole heaven clasping the whole earth, and dwarfed the difficulties of terrestrial roads into mere patches on a map.

As has been said, the sphere of this special association was limited. I have carefully stated its nature and extent, because I do not wish to be understood as claiming any special authority outside of it for the account here given. Not only his own family, but many others of his friends, unquestionably enjoyed more intimate and frequent association with him than was my lot. In the one particular field I have named, however, I have reason to believe he had no other constant companion than myself. And, in some respects, this circumstance afforded peculiar opportunities for observing his mental habits and methods. Whether these glimpses revealed the whole, may indeed be questioned. I think that what they did reveal was really characteristic of *him*, and not merely of the occasions when they were given. It must be remembered, however, that such analysis as I was able to make applies to his later life only. How much of the result may be ascribed to age and habit, I shall not here discuss. It is an interesting question, upon which a good deal could be said.

Mr. Beecher himself overestimated, in my judgment, my intellectual comprehension of him. He inferred too hastily from intuitive recognitions of single points, a thorough acquaintance. But I knew better; for all my reconnaissances put together would not make a map of him.

He came to me once, saying, "—— asks me who can write some articles about me for a book he thinks of publishing. He has several contributions promised; but I have told him that if he wants anybody to tell him *how my mind works*, he must come to you." I refused to do this, even at his request, on the double ground that I did not know as much as he fancied, and that, in any case, I would not do it while he lived.

Before that, however, I had once written at his request, in the German language, an account of his life, with some analysis of the sources of his power, to serve as an introduction to a German translation of "Life Thoughts", "Royal Truths", and a selection of sermons, published in three volumes at Berlin, in 1870. The result of this performance was amusing enough. Mr. Beecher forwarded my manuscript to the translator, vouching, I suppose, for its substantial accuracy. In due time the books appeared; and we found ourselves dressed and posed in the most amazing fashion. The worthy preacher at Frankfort-on-the-Oder who had translated the sermons and extracts with fair, albeit somewhat clumsy fidelity, seemed to have felt himself entitled to use with greater freedom the manuscript material furnished by Mr. Beecher's friend, which he had interwoven with opinions and reflections of his own, and complemented with an extraordinary account of Brooklyn and Plymouth church, derived, Heaven knows whence. Here are a few specimen paragraphs:

"In Brooklyn about 100 newspapers appear daily. The streets of Brooklyn are built at right angles. They run in endless straight lines. There are railroads in all of them, much used during the week. But it is Sunday when we land. All the streets are closed with great iron chains. Nowhere an omnibus, carriage, cab, milk-wagon or saddle-horse. We must resolve, like all the aristocratic Yankees, to make our way to church on foot. The deep mud and the miserable pavement oblige us at intervals to carry our ladies literally in our arms. . . . . Not to miss the shortest way, we beg a good woman who passes with a book in her hand, to direct us to the church of the Congregationalists. 'Nothing easier,' replies the old lady, smiling amiably; 'pay no attention to the churches on the left. The church of the Congregationalists is on your right. On that side you have simply to go by twenty-three churches and chapels. The twenty-fourth building, standing about in the middle of the street, is the Congregational church.' With thanks, we begin our journey to the church — in single file on account of the mud. At every hundred paces a Greek, Byzantine or gothic edifice lifts proudly to heaven its tower or dome. We have already passed the twentieth street. Everywhere sabbath stillness. From no quarter sounds an audible word. All doors are shut.

" .... We read on the corner the prosaic name, '53d street'; and before us stands in its full proportions the marble temple of the Congregationalists, erected twenty-two years ago.

"We enter. No altar, no organ, no pulpit, no pictures, no flowers, no lights. The church is crowded. There are some three thousand present. The deepest stillness reigns. At last there appears behind a desk, which stands on the same level as the audience, a tall, broad-shouldered man in ordinary dress (the clerical coat is unknown in America) with a black neck-tie. It is the preacher. .... Immediately there arises from all the benches a melody, softer than the sighing of the wind upon the waves. .... Not all the Plymouth churches pray singing. In the Brooklyn church Beecher introduced it after a long, fierce struggle."

And so on, and so on! Mr. Beecher's merriment over this description may be imagined. It was perhaps more annoying to his ambitious young biographer, who found himself, in the same pages, cited with florid compliment as an authority, and thus made apparently responsible for the marble temple in the middle of the street, and other fantastic novelties. Mr. Beecher presented the book to me, as a memento of my literary undertaking, and slily suggested that either I had presumed on his ignorance of German, and smuggled all that stuff into the manuscript, the contents of which I had pretended to translate to him before he accepted it, or else my German was so bad that this was all the editor could make out of it! As to correcting the misstatements of the pious translator, he said it was better to let such things take care of themselves.

After this unexpectedly long and desultory introduction, I will set down simply the peculiar aspects of Mr. Beecher's mental activity, so far as it was exhibited to me. On other occasions, I have mentioned some of them, and have also sketched essential traits of his character and beliefs, as I had learned to know them. But the latter view will not be taken now. The extracts of which this book is composed will, to some extent, constitute a self-revelation of him. Perhaps the hints I give may help the reader to understand and harmonize them.

The first peculiarity in the action of Mr. Beecher's mind was its periodicity. As I have elsewhere explained, he had three distinct mental states: the receptive and inquiring or filling-up, the spontaneously productive or creative, and the passive or resting state. The third was a reaction from the second. In it, he loved to be alone with birds, flowers, gems, pictures — things, in short, that asked no questions, and called for no active reciprocities. He welcomed, also, the company of little children, or of friends who would let him alone, and not try to "draw him out". If these conditions were not fulfilled, he would often depart suddenly without explanation or farewell.

His productive state was, in its nature, the fitful mood of genius; but he had studied its conditions so thoroughly and he followed its laws so consistently as to have it under control to a degree unparalleled, I believe, among men of equal power. Apart from all his innumerable other activities, he carried the consciousness that every Sunday must, if possible, find him in this state; and he so arranged the physical and mental strains of the preceding days as to bring it about with astonishing regularity.

No doubt it was the result of lifelong habit that this productive activity seldom lasted for more than two hours. Probably in his younger days, he could remain under its influence longer, or recover from its reaction more quickly. But as I knew him, two hours' work in speaking or in writing was usually all that he could do without repose aud recovery — mainly through silence and sleep. From one to two hours had been for so many years the customary period of his supreme effort in speech or sermon, or writing of editorials or "Star papers", and he had so thoroughly trained himself to prepare for that period and to relapse from it without further waste of strength, that at last he could scarcely command his own powers in any other way. I have known him on an occasion — not public — calling for more prolonged continuous labor, to lose the thread of his thought, forget scenes and incidents, and be obliged to suspend all efforts at renewal until the following day. Moreover, it was not easy then to resume the broken argument, until by some fortunate hint an association of ideas was aroused, and the previous mental condition was instantly reproduced — after which, there was no further difficulty. He used to describe such an experience as the clouding of his view, after a certain period of intense and keen perception, by a mist or shade closing in upon it, and the subsequent lifting or parting of this vail, and revelation of the original scene unchanged. But it was not always the former scene that thus returned — perhaps never, unless it were a simple picture of memory, and even then, though the haze of mental obscuration might have been removed, some further impulse might be necessary, as in the illustration just given, to flash before the eye the vision it had had and lost. For all events, conversations, and processes of his own thought which stood connected with particular scenes, his memory, once aroused, was accurate, even to minute details. On the other hand, he could not quote from memory, or, as a general rule, trace to its origin any idea which he had once received and made his own.

Not only the conscious action of Mr. Beecher's memory, but the operations of creative conception and utterance in his productive mood, were dependent upon a sort of space-association. His conclusions were "views", in an almost literal sense. According to his own account, his fine sermons, before he preached them, lay before him like a wide prospect, perfectly defined in every part. It was not until an aspect of truth, taking shape slowly and by degrees in his mind, spread itself at last thus complete before him, that he was ready to express it in a sermon. Both the argument and the illustrations were usually thus foreseen.

In the final act of utterance, another mental operation was involved — the construction of sentences and the choice of words. But here, also, the pictorial or scenic conception of his theme controlled and assisted him. For he was always simply translating and declaring what he saw, and never pretending to see what he labored to describe. The result was a singular felicity of style, and freedom from such rhetorical blemishes as "mixed figures" or false transitions.

It must be added, however, that the force, fluency and beauty of language which he had at command were distinctly the product of immense reading, conducted (especially in earlier years) for this particular end. Even at a recent period, he named to me authors whom he said he read because they brought him words, not specially because they gave him valuable thoughts or facts. Several times I have been surprised to find him reading with apparent zest essays or romances which no critic would place in the first rank. "How can you bear such turgid 'fine writing'?" I said once. "It's a gorgeous vocabulary," was his reply; "and I want it!" Putting many things together, I can perceive that his later reading, being, to so large an extent, among philosophical, psychological and scientific books, tended to crowd him into the precise but narrow nomenclature which these employ; and he turned to vivid narrators, even to sophomoric spouters, as a corrective. Some criticisms of books which I find in his letters show that he fully appreciated clearness and simplicity of statement; but when, with a special purpose, he was "reading for words", his taste was oratorical. He would then enjoy a style which belonged to the platform rather than the printed page, although he knew well enough that it was a bad style. At a certain stage of his life, as many will remember, he freely employed the terms of phrenology; but as subsequent studies brought him to a point where he could no longer hold the theories of phrenology, the words expressive of those theories were unconsciously abandoned — a striking illustration of the manner in which he used language wholly as a means of expression.

In the vehemence of extempore speech, he was often not able to make selection among his own thoughts. Whatever was in him, as part of the panoramic conception of his theme, was likely to take fire and blaze up with the rest. But in the selection of words to express his thought, he exercised a perpetual and subtle choice. Even here, his conception was pictorial. "Words!" said he, one day; "when I am well started, I don't need to hunt for words! They come in crowds, getting in one another's way, and each one saying, 'Take me! take me!'"

Close observation of the process of his choosing among words has shown it to differ in rapidity, rather than kind, from that of ordinary men. What we do, when, pen in hand, we mentally ransack our recollections of synonymous and related terms, or when we consult (mostly in vain) somebody's *Thesaurus*, he did instantly and automatically, marshalling before him by unconscious summons the whole host at once. It was often noticeable that they trooped in etymological bands, and according to primitive root-sounds and root-meanings. Few men have ever so completely transformed classical culture into a critical appreciation of the mother-tongue. While Mr. Beecher, so far as I ever knew, read, after middle life, little or no Latin and Greek, no one who minutely observed his language could doubt that he had studied both, and that English words brought before his swift perception their origins, and therefore their essential meanings and degrees of fitness and force. With this intimate knowledge of them was coupled an educated and exquisite feeling for the association of sound with sense. He used strong Saxon words, when they were the right words; but he had none of that affected Saxon simplicity which takes the resonance out of Bryant's Homer. His favorite prose writer, John Milton, was not less afraid of Latin words than he, if they carried the melodious thunder he desired, and added rich historic significance to their immediate message.

It was amusing, sometimes, to watch his impetuous dash after a word — getting it, as it were, by the collar, as he prolonged the *s* or *m*, or other root-initial, until the resisting captive was forced to come out of the crowd altogether. Often he would make such a dash after a word which should by analogy exist, but did not; and then he would create a new word out of the root-form with which he had started, or the vivid picture behind it. Instances of this sort were more frequent than the printed reports of his sermons (especially revised reports) will show. Such expressions as, "He sends to care for them his *mothering* angels"; "a great, big, *carbunculous* lie"; "mean, wriggling, *vermicular* men," etc., sprang from embarrassments of this or an analogous sort. Here, also, it may be remarked, that the process itself was not unique; but its rapidity and audacity were so.

In many, perhaps in most cases, the panoramic "view" or conception of Mr. Beecher was not broadly recognizable by his audience, because, as a general rule, he ended a sermon leaving much unsaid. This could be easily proved by inspecting his rough notes. Almost always they indicated aspects and applications which were omitted for lack of time in delivery. He habitually limited himself to an hour in preaching; and as the hand of the clock approached that period, made haste to a conclusion, which was usually, in obedience to oratorical instinct, a true peroration in form. But deeper analysis would show how really incomplete was the exposition thus artistically rounded to a close. Strictly speaking, it was, in most cases, the "application" rather than the exposition proper, which was cut short. His sermons were usually built on one plan: First, a statement of the truth; then, the enforcement of the duty. But the preliminary statement often involved the application; and the subsequent use of the doctrine often illumined the definition of it. So, after all, there was something lost under both heads when the clock cut short the preacher.

Mr. Beecher used to say that he was, in the presence of an audience, an entirely different person from what he was as a private individual; that he felt conscious of a relation of authority and power, which forsook him when he came down the pulpit-stairs. "I am, in private," he said, "though you may not think it, constitutionally shy and reserved; often inexplicably afraid to speak; seized with reluctance or fear, even upon entering a room. But when I face an audience it is all gone. In that mood, I cannot be daunted or disconcerted. If the house took fire, I would order the crowd to go out quietly; and they would, too! It is a different life altogether!"

This sketch of his productive state is far from complete, even as a summary of the partial study upon which it is based; but I must content myself with but one additional touch. Mr. Beecher's prayers, considered purely as revelations of mental processes, confirm the foregoing statements. Being wholly unstudied and spontaneous, they give, indeed, the most valuable evidence of all concerning the workings of his mind. Proceeding, evidently, from personal experience and emotion, they may be searched almost in vain for any expression so peculiarly personal that it cannot be realized, adopted and employed by a multitude of worshippers. Moses, always carrying his people on his heart, even in the awful loneliness of his intercourse with Jehovah, was not more truly conscious of his representative position than these prayers indicate Mr. Beecher to have been. Liturgies, or those dry recitals of commonplace petitions which have the monotony of liturgies without their music and grace and dear associations, are, of course, appropriately collective in character; but the marvel here is, that in infinite variety and with the perfect freedom of solitary prayer, the individual soul utters itself so that all souls can—nay, must—take part. If we seek the explanation in the structure of these prayers, we shall find that, almost without exception, each of them consists essentially of a "view" of God— a view which all can have who will take the same standpoint of trust, gratitude and joy. This view being expressed, the prayer concludes with a few general petitions more conventional in character and form. The real heart of the prayer, its communion and its exalting power.are in the "view".

Something must be said about that one of Mr. Beecher's states of mind which, though enumerated first, has been left to the last. I mean his inquiring, studying, filling-up mood. This was, in fact, the one in which he passed most of his waking hours. The supreme efforts of production and the relapses of exhaustion did not compare in duration with the periods of eager, inquisitive, observant and reflective accumulation. He was like one of the reservoirs employed in some of our western mining districts in the variety of hydraulic mining known as "booming". The gates being opened, a tremendous torrent rushes out, and does its brief work mightily; then the reservoir lies empty for a little while; then, the gates being shut, the water of a thousand rivulets is gathered again for a new exhibition of power.

Nothing came amiss to Mr. Beecher's gathering mood. He did not go hunting for particular things (except as he did it in pursuing some special line of reading); he questioned everything. He studied all occupations and trades, until he had learned what chords to strike that would echo in the bosom of each different class of his fellow-men. He studied men, in order to gain influence over them; and while his inexhaustible credulity of goodness, believing all things and hoping all things, often betrayed him in individual judgments, his knowledge of human nature was marvelous, and for the purpose for which he acquired and used it, well-nigh unerring.

The thoughts, facts, illustrations and impulses thus accumulated, seemed to lie in his mind as if in a solution, slowly crystallizing into new forms. Some day he would have a "view"; and then the result of long pondering would suddenly appear. As I have said, he tried to save his mood of utterance for the occasions when utterance was a public duty. But he was sometimes roused to it in private. Then it made no difference whether the audience were many or few. He became the inspired orator. I remember several occasions of this kind, when he poured out grand and beautiful expositions of truth, which never recurred afterwards to his thought. He moved on, and those particular views were not visible from any other summit.

Of books in which he was really interested, he was a slow and careful reader. I think he rarely marked them with marginal comments in words; but I have frequently found in those which he lent to me dashes and scorings, indicating passages to which he wished to turn again for further study, or which he regarded as specially significant. The only case I can recall in which he marked a book of mine is that of "Lorna Doone". He borrowed the story, and kept it for some time, frequently expressing his delight in its minute descriptions of nature. After he had returned it, I found written in it the following admirable criticism:

"This book is like a capital fowl, well cooked — somewhat

over-stuffed with delicacies, and possibly, a trifle too long in the oven; otherwise, a dish fit for a king."

Turning from these attempts to sketch a single "view" of this many-sided character, let me conclude with one or two brief hints, suggested by it, which may be useful to the readers of the passages collected in this book.

1. Remember that each of these fragments, so far as it states a proposition or opinion, is probably part of a larger "view", and that a full, systematic statement of Mr. Beecher's opinions cannot be made by piecing together these fragments out of their original perspective relations. If his own more extended statements were but single views, these portions of them are only glimpses.

2. Remember that the dominant purpose back of all these utterances was to help and to win men. They do not analyze truth, as a chemist might analyze a drug, but exhibit it, as (in the old-fashioned phrase) a physician "exhibits" a medicine. This is the immemorial attitude of the preacher toward the truth. Mr. Beecher used to say that half the controversies of theology came from the attempt to interpret as universal and complete propositions what Paul said to meet individual cases. He was in this, as in many other particulars, like Paul. However wide and grand the vision before him, he was always showing it to somebody, and emphasizing those features of it which he desired that person or class of persons to perceive and feel. "I must aim at some one," he said; "then I shall reach, perhaps, some other one. But if I aim at everybody, I shall hit nobody."

3. Do not rest in the shallow notion that these are the mere coruscations of intellectual electricity — the flashes of poetic genius — the heat of a blazing sympathy only. Even in these broken lights may be discovered the steady glow of deep and devout thought. Mr. Beecher was not superficial or reckless; his grasp of great mental and spiritual problems was not the light touch of a decorative artist or a dallying connoisseur. It is worth while to seek beneath the brilliancy of his wit and eloquence, even beneath the flowing current of his sympathy, for the profounder, eternal meaning — the word of God, spoken by the mouth of a prophet.   ROSSITER W. RAYMOND.

THE CROWN OF LIFE.

THE first grand element of liberty is a heart transformed unto the temperature of heaven, unto the Divine benevolence, so that a man shall not be so sensitive about himself nor about the future of his own name, nor about his standing, nor about the opposition he may bring upon himself, nor about anything that is low and personal whatsoever, but may hold all his rights in the sublime and most beautiful temperature of universal benevolence and Christian love.

A man is free just in proportion to the number of natural or social laws that he has learned to obey. For a man is of himself very little; but he has learnt the courses of God in Nature and employs them, and he rides upon the sea or by steam upon land, and goes swifter than the bird; but in every case it is because he has rendered himself subject to some or many natural laws. Instead of liberty consisting in an unharnessed freedom, liberty consists, in its largest estate and greatest variety, in obedience to the greatest number of social, moral, and civil laws. "Take My yoke upon you, that you may be free; carry My burden, that you may be light."

*
* *

The way to emancipate a man is to make him so large that you can't afford to furnish iron enough to make a fetter.

*
* *

A perfect Christian is the one and only creature that has absolute liberty unchecked by law, by institution, by foregoing thoughts of men, by public sentiment. Because a perfect man is in unison with the Divine soul, he has the whole liberty of God in himself, according to the measure of his manhood. But he has liberty to do only what he wants to do, and he wants to do nothing that is not within the bounds and benefit of a pure and true love. He becomes a law to himself; that is, he carries in himself that inspiration of love which is the mother of all good law. He is higher than any law. For you and for me, riding across country, there are metes and bounds, fences, rivers, ditches; but for birds there are none. They fly higher. For low men, low-toned, there are metes and bounds of custom and public sentiment or institutions, laws and restrictions; but for one who has gone up higher than all these into the universal and divine, there are no such things. He thinks what is true, he does what is benevolent. His will is with God's will. He has liberty, not to do anything on his own judgment and desire, but anything that is not contrary to reason, conscience, and the desire of a soul wholly controlled by the spirit of love, which is the spirit of Christ.

You cannot put men together as you put together a carpenter's logs when he has hewn and jointed them. Society has to be made up of free men, and a free man is a largely branched man all around. That government is coming more and more into vogue which rejoices in diversity, and which merely says that one man's liberty shall not prevent another man's liberty, but that he shall accommodate himself and his neighbor likewise.

Men's rights are a great deal of trouble to them. They assert them and get them, and then they don't know what to do with them. A man's rights, half of them, are meant to give away.

The beatitude of your rights is, they are your benevolences. You can yield them, give them away. And the law of social unity is this law of assertion of a man's individuality, and the use of that individuality as a benevolence for those that are around him.

The letters that spell *rights* are the letters that spell *duties*.

* *

The supreme conception of manhood is that of a vital spirit full of voluntary action; full of unrestrained will; full of thought, flying high and free as the winds fly, and profuse as the flowers of spring. God's spirit developes a thousand times more bountifully from the human soil than the sun does from the natural soil, all vines, all shrubs, all high growing trees, all lowly plants, grass, moss, everything in its place, and of its kind.

It is this multifarious spontaniety in man that constitutes the grandeur of manhood; and it is this spontaniety that men try to repress by institutions, by denominations, by sects, by authority in its different forms, hewing off the branches here and there. But liberty is one of the signs of Christianity; by as much as a man is a craven and trembles before his priest, by so much is he less a Christian.

By as much as a man is superstitious about Sundays, about ordinances, about forms and ceremonies, by so much is his Christian character weakened. He that loves God until he fears nothing is the typical Christian—the ideal man; and out of him proceed all kindness, all truth, all love, all faith, all self-respect, all needful restraint, all things that go to make him a full man, moving in the ranks of society easily and naturally.

* * *

No man is so free as that man who has accepted the law of God which is expressed in the words, "Thou shalt love God supremely and thy neighbor as thyself." There is no sound in the universe that cannot be chorded to that. Love is the only true concert-pitch. Let pride be the concert-pitch, and you cannot bring the orchestra of human nature into agreement with it. Let taste be the concert-pitch, and you cannot make all the other faculties of a man harmonize with it. There is many a part of our being with which all the other parts cannot be made concordant. But sound the word *love* —love to God and man—and there is no passion or appetite, there is no taste, there is no social feeling, there is no intellectual element, there is no moral sentiment, that cannot be brought into perfect accord with it—yea, and be made nobler and better by it.

* * *

Rights increase as man increases—and as the man increases not merely in physical stature or in skill of manual employment or material strength, but in character. So as men work up higher and higher toward the Divine standard of character their rights and liberties increase.

A true life in Jesus Christ is a life of liberty, of largeness, of joyfulness and peacefulness, and if a man wants to get the most out of the life that he is living in this world it is better that he should reap the crop out of the top of his head and not out of the bottom of it.

What sanctity there is in loves and friendships that have found their way up into the crystal dome!

To love one is to hold the heavens behind him, his faults and failings being cast upon the background of the immortality of love. What power is there in souls thus drawn together by mutual sympathy and helpfulness, whose very life is the exaltation of the spiritual life of each!

Whoever has kindled in him that feeling of affection by which he devotes his whole life to the filling up of other people's lives, has the beginning of the knowledge of God — that is, of its higher elements and nobler attributes. Nobody can come even into the outer court of this understanding but he comes through some reciprocity, some echo of God in his own self.

No one has true love who does not know that it is

the inspiration of nobility; that it is a power which is carrying its object upward, being willing to suffer for the sake of lifting it higher and higher. That is the test of man's love, because God has given it to us as the test of His own love.

*
* *

A child at the foot of a mountain and a father at the top cannot see alike. The child is embosomed in shrubs and trees, and is enveloped in darkness; the sun comes to the valley where he is, long after it strikes the mountain-top; it passes from the child's sight far earlier than it does from the father's; and the view of the surrounding country which the child gets below is not to interpret that which the father gets above. So our conception of finite love is not to interpret God's conception of infinite love. How little do we understand perfect love, infinite love, out of which all the universe is born, by which it is governed, which converts pain and sorrow to helpful uses! Earthly love is most beautiful, to be sure; it is as yet uncrowned. But what is the love of the Infinite? What is love to a heart that can take in ages and the race? What is that love which is unfathomable, and which includes infinite tenderness and infinite compassion?

*
* *

Love is the true alchemy that can change everything into gold.

* * *

A love that penetrates as a perfume does; that never sleeps; that divides every thought or feeling of joy and sorrow; that turns service to regency; that makes pain a pleasure; that is always growing; that in the loved one's absence fills all life with his image, and his presence obliterates the whole world beside; that with him makes the desert wilderness a garden, and without him changes Eden into a barren croft; that lives in him, and without him dies—who does not know that such a great love is possible? I do not say that every one has found it in his own experience, but I think that every one must be impoverished that has not known such love; sometimes worthily bestowed and sometimes unworthily. This power of love is given by God to men; and there is nothing like it, either for beauty or for majesty.

The love which is the basis and the sum of Christianity is something grander than any specialization of affection known to man. Nor is there, if peradventure it do not somewhat exist in the household, anything that is fit to be type of that which the Spirit of God teaches us to be the love of Christianity. For it is not a mild and feeble amiableness; it is not a kind of charity that forgives men's faults, and has no conscience rebounding from evil. It is not merely morality, indifferent to everything that is not regular, and without any quick sense of good or evil, of the beauty of the one and the odiousness of the other. It is large, robust, discriminating, full of rectitude itself and the love of rectitude, full of moral discrimination, repulsed from evil and attracted to all that is beautiful and true and good. It is the whole man attuned to God's own nature, and therefore full of sympathy, full of kindness, full of fervent well-wishing to all sentient creatures. It does not disdain the flitting insect, nor flocks and herds, nor the birds that build and sing; but it has its full disclosure among men. It is that quality which shines out with beneficence on all.

It asks nothing for itself; it has no second thought; it asks only the liberty of bestowing kindness and affection and sympathy and all helpfulness. It sees faults, longing to correct them; it sees sins, that it may heal them; it is the soul's physician going into the hospital where men are maimed and are sick, only to see how they may be succored and helped. It is the soul's whole atmosphere poured forth upon others. Thus it is not a faculty; it is all the faculties and forces of the soul in a condition of imparting benefit, at any rate well-wishing, to all creatures. And thus it is a miniature of God set up in the niche of our soul.

Love is the pendulum of the universe.

***

The love is very vulgar that only thinks and traffics. "You love me and I love you." What is that better than, "Here is gold, give me some lace; here is money, give me that picture?" It is mere trafficking. "You don't love me, you don't care anything about me, and I'm not going to care anything about you." Here are the quarrels of love, here are the dramas written and unwritten, and there are millions more unwritten, than ever were written. Here is the scale. Is there not a love that is expressed by the Apostle, "Though the more I love the less am I loved, I glory in that; I know I love more than you do; I know that I am not much loved, that makes no difference; you may not love me nor care for me, nor sympathize with me; but I love you." It is the power of love without reciprocation. And the greatest natures have that power. They do not love faults or failings, but the people that bear them they love. And love takes its measure out of the soul from which it comes; its magnitude, its purity, and its beauty are determined by the lover, not by the recipient.

Love is the fulfilling of the law. It is the central crystallization for character. No matter how strong the variant parts of a man's conflicting nature, if once they all consent to take the law of love and bow down in allegiance to it, you have harmonized the character, and the harmonization of it makes it strong by the amount of its differences.

. The love of the mother is but one drop of the ocean

as compared with the love of the great Father of mankind — infinite, infinite!

* * *

The only slave on God's earth that needs no compassion and pity is the slave of love.

* * *

No man knows true happiness till he has learned how to love — how to love not a little, but a great deal; how to love not occasionally, as a sweetmeat at a banquet, but how so to love that he is tied up by it, he is in bondage to it, it rules him.

* * *

Great is the power of love. But if this be so where the object is unworthy, what must it be where the object transcends all conception; where it is more multitudinous in its beauty than are the fields with all their flowers in all the seasons; where every day the horizon of his nobleness swings wider; where every day there dawns some new star of his virtues and his excellence? O! cast away your crowns and your scepters. There is no palace like the soul. There is no coronation like that which love gives and takes when a great soul not only has loved, but has loved to redemption. If a woman was in early days ill-bred and perverted, and has gone wrong, upon compulsion or persuasion, and secretly hungering and thirsting after righteousness, is still snared and imprisoned, and fast being degraded, but is at last by some kindly ministration brought out of temptation, and is learning, growing, revolting from every evil thought or feeling, her whole horizon clearing from every cloud or taint, rising to an unexpected beauty and dignity; and if, in some day, royal above every other day, she shall hear him say, "Oh! mine elect, I have chosen thee to be the companion of my life; thou art mine!" What amazement! Flooded with tears, and paralyzed with surprise, she answers, "It cannot be; it cannot be. I should be but a blemish to thee." But he replies: "I have found thee, I have redeemed thee, and I will continue to keep thee; thou art mine." Who can estimate the wonder of that soul, lifting itself up in loving adoration upon him who is worthy to be the object of every thought and affection, who has loved her, and who has given himself for her, and to her?

That is the love of redemption. That is the love of the soul that has been found of Christ, and has been pardoned and lifted up into life and light. That is the love which cries out in a moment of ecstasy, "Whom have I in heaven but thee? and there is none upon earth that I desire beside thee." This is the great love of the ransomed soul for Jesus Christ; and out of that experience comes the walking day by day in the faith that says, "I know that my Redeemer liveth; I know that I am loved of Him, and that I love Him with all my heart; the life that I live in the flesh, I live by that faith." Out of such an experience as that, what strength springs, what peace, what rejoicing, what gladness! With that, one hardly needs to go to heaven; it is heaven on earth.

A love, a sentiment, comes as a wave comes, and subsides, and rolls back, as a wave rolls into the bosom of the great unexhausted sea.

Love on earth is as dry husks compared with the glory of the ever-living and ever-glowing love of God. Love is atonement, and God is love.

In some natures Love is born of Peace, nourished in tranquility, and from the first brings forth joy and peace. It knows no struggle, but only gradual development. But in other natures, Love has a controlling work to perform before it may rule in peace. Like a stream born in the mountains, it hides itself among rocks, it is driven over them in foam and fury, it is shut up in dark pools, and steals away through ravines and cliffs, still gathering power but finding no quiet until, far away from its sources, it has fulfilled its course; and then at length, its pure waters, flowing through flower-breeding meadows, rest in deep lakes, where all its agitations are forgotten in deep tranquility. Not one star that shone upon it all the way down the mountain could reflect again except in torn and scattered beams of light. Now every star of heaven is at home in its bosom.

⁎

First comes acquaintance — that is May; then friendship — that is June; then brother and sisterhood — that is July; and then love — that is August; but July and August are so much alike that no one can tell where one stops and the other begins.

⁎

In a full and large nature, friendliness is but the outer court, love is the holy of holies. Into that enters only the ordained of God.

⁎

Royalty and Fortune have no light to fill the vault of life when love is eclipsed or has gone down. But if love be regent every other light may go out and it will fill the life with a light that shall make poverty itself luminous, and sickness and toil bright and joyous.

⁎

Getting in love is like picking garden flowers in the night. You may get a violet, or you may pick a nettle.

⁎

The whole New Testament pivots on the golden

point, "Thou shalt love." At twelve o'clock at night, from out of a hundred or a thousand steeples goes forth the solemn bell, striking the last hours; and every one of them strikes twelve — some in tenor tone, some in deep, resounding bass, and with every variation of pure tone or clangour, but every one of them strikes at the hour this one sovereign note, "Love" — some one way, some in another, some through emotion, some organized, some disorganized; but every one of the great truths of the New Testament strikes Love.

You cannot tell the strength of one's love by the pleasure which he receives from loving. The test of loving is what one is willing to suffer for the sake of the object beloved. All deep love takes the object, as it were, into its bosom; carries its burdens, or would; forgives its sin, or would; suffers. Any man that has nobody to suffer for him in this world is God's orphan indeed.

The sentiment of the soul, the throb of love — though it has no voice with which to sing, no language with which to orate, no treasure with which to build, no hand cunning and curious in carving a structure, the simple impulse in the soul of love to God and love to men, is not barren nor unfruitful. In the sight of God it has the chiefest value.

There is no spendthrift like the heart. It does not know economy, it will not learn, but gives all, always.

Great souls have bled to death because they did not know where to bestow the precious gift of love. One may be conscious of being worthy to be loved, but still more conscious of having wonderful stores of love to pour forth, and yet be starved all the while.

Christ represents God and is Divine. He came forth into this world, not merely to make declarations of truth, but to live them; to put them into the form of conduct, so that wherever He went men looking on Him might say, "This is the interpretation."

I find no difficulty in saying Christ is God, because I never undertake to weigh God with scales or to measure Him with compasses.

There are men who have sat down and figured God out; they have figured up the matters of omnipotence, of omniscience and of omnipresence; they have marked the limits to which Divine power can go; they can tell why God may do so and so, and why He may not do this, that or the other; and I can understand how they should raise objections to saying Christ is God.

I draw out from my pocket a little miniature, and look upon it, and tears drop from my eyes. What is it? A piece of ivory. What is on it? A face some artist has painted there. It is a radiant face. My history is connected with it. When I look upon it tides of feeling swell in me. Some one comes to me and says, "What is that?" I say, "It is my mother." "Your mother! I should call it a piece of ivory with water-colors on it." To me it is my mother. When you come to scratch it and analyze it and scrutinize the elements of it, to be sure it is only a sign or dumb show, but it brings to me that which is no sign nor dumb show. According to the law of my mind, through it I have brought back, interpreted, refreshed, revived, made potent in me, all the sense of what a loving mother was.

So I take my conception of Christ as he is painted in dead letters on dead paper; and to me is interpreted the glory, the sweetness, the patience, the love, the joy-inspiring nature of God; and I do not hesitate to say, "Christ is my God", just as I would not hesitate to say of that picture, "It is my mother".

When, therefore, Christ is presented to me I will not put Him in the multiplication table, I will not make Him a problem in arithmetic or in mathematics; I will not stand and say, "How can three be one or how can one be three?" I will interpret Christ by the imagination and the heart. Then He will bring me a conception of God such as the heavens never, in all their glory, declared; such as the earth has never revealed, either in ancient or modern times. He reveals to us a God whose interest in man is inherent, and who, through His mercy and goodness made sacrifices for it. God so loved the world that He gave His only begotten Son to die for it. What is the only begotten Son of God? Who knows? Who cares to know? That His only begotten Son is precious to Him we may know, judging from the experience of an earthly father; and we cannot doubt that when He gave Christ to come into life, and humble Himself to man's condition, and take upon Himself an ignominious death, He sacrificed that which was exceedingly dear to Him. And this act is a revelation of the feeling of God toward the human race.

I do not measure my God by outwardness, but by the substance of the inward life, by wisdom, by love, and all the fruit of love; and if Jesus Christ is not of the nature of God, then I have lost all conception of what that can possibly be. He represents to me the very highest attribute of God. I do not count the stilling of the waves as being so very Divine, or if it is, it is the little finger of God; but when Jesus Christ can suffer that other men might not suffer; when He developed the idea that God's nature was that of one who had rather that He should Himself take the bondage and burden; when He showed paternal feeling beyond father and mother, that had rather suffer in the family than that the child should suffer, then I begin to say, "Here is love; here is light". If the questions that I would fain propose are not questions to be solved — namely, how He could be God and yet man — I remit those questions to theology; and to a very large extent theology is the vast abyss into which men throw things that they cannot deal with in any other way. To me Jesus is the exposition outwardly of the inward life of God, and I follow Him everywhere on earth, and I say, "This is God, this is God, and this is God"; and I free from my thoughts as one frees a weight from the soul, I free the earthly circumstances of Christ's life. And then I say, "This is the trait, this is the quality, this is the Divine nature"; and then I enthrone it in the Father, I enthrone it in the Holy Ghost, and the whole earth doth show forth what the centre of the universe is. Yes; I believe in the Divinity of Christ because I believe in God, and because in Him alone can I gain any adequate conception of what is the sum and centre of God himself.

Therefore I am not turned back from believing in the Trinity because I cannot comprehend it. When you ask me as to the *quo modo*, the method, of the Trinity, I am obliged to confess that I do not understand it. But should this be a bar to my going into the church? A certain phase of orthodoxy says, "You must subscribe to the Trinity, or not come into the church". What is the law on which it proceeds, and by which it judges a man? Is it simplicity? Is it transparency? Is it lovableness? Is it that on which the fifth chapter of Matthew is founded? No. Men go into the most unfathomable realms of human thought, take the most difficult of all conceivable speculations, and make them the condition of church-membership; and if a man believes in them he may be in the church, but if he does not believe in them he shall not be in the church.

I believe in the Lord Jesus Christ with all my heart and soul as my Saviour and my hope of everlasting life. I believe in Him so that life itself is stained through and through to me with Jesus Christ.

The doctrine of the presence of God everywhere, in all, as the one great force that is working in nature and in human life, is nowhere so significantly taught as by Jesus and recorded by John. He is not a God that has invented the world and stands like an engineer to see how it runs; not a God afar off, a mechanical God; not an architectural God, a builder that does not live in his own building; but a God universally diffused, to such an extent that wherever there is force, there is God behind that force. Though Agnostic and Atheistic reasoners should rename God, and call Him "Force" or "Energy", I care not; if by that they mean, as they must, what we mean by "Jehovah", by "Lord", by "God", they can make a name to suit themselves. The name is not the thing, but the qualities that are under it.

* * *

Jesus Christ epitomizes, represents, interprets God to us as the central fountain, source and supply of transcendent benevolence and love in the universe. This intense interest and love in God works to the development of every soul toward Him. It is not divine indifference. It is not divine good-nature. It is not divine passivity. It is a parent's desire for a child's development from evil toward goodness, toward purity, toward sweetness, toward godliness. God is one who is laborious and self-sacrificing, seeking the race, not because they are so good, but to make them good, stimulating them, inspiring them, and desiring above all things else that they shall be fashioned away from the animal toward His sonship. That is the direction and drift of divine government.

* * *

What art thou, O Sun? Thou that bringest back from captivity the winter day; thou that teaches all the dead things in the earth to find themselves again; thou that dost drive the night away from the weary eyes of watchers, thou that art the universal bounty-giver; thou that dost travel endlessly, carrying benefactions immeasurable, illimitable, beyond want and conception of want—thou art the figure that represents God; and God is as much greater in bounty and mercy and power than thou art as spirit is greater than matter. For the sun is a spark. Around about the brow of Him that reigns are suns sparkling as jewels in a crown. What, then, is that God who is accustomed to speak of himself to us as the Sun of Righteousness, that arises with healing in his beams?

When you lift the Lord Jesus Christ up before men, remember that, with a certain constancy, He is as various as the heavens. We in the temperate zone know that during winter and summer the same skies are over our heads; but did you ever notice how the seasons vary? No two springs ever walked the earth with the same sandals. No two weeks were ever precisely the same. No day is the exact copy of any other day. The sun, I suppose, never rises as it has risen before. I suppose the sun never sets twice alike. That Artist of artists, who reaches forth His hands, profuse with color, and makes pictures hemispheric, continental, never repeats Himself. He paints figures of majesty and glory on the sky. He piles clouds in grandeur, like mountain ranges, upon the horizon. He wipes out the wrinkles of His cloud-painting, and lets the sun go down unobscured. The scene is always changing. It is never just what it has been, and we forever exclaim, "It is beautiful!" Now the Sun of Righteousness, Jesus, the Lord, is never one fixed thing.

There are some men whose God is like the moon as we sometimes see it painted on clocks, with a round, fixed face, behind which the machinery ticks, ticks, ticks, without cessation, and which always looks alike. Idolators are they. For the true God is from everlasting to everlasting the inspirational God, whose thoughts win all thoughts, and of whom we are but dying sparks. Every heart here has some slight touch of the divine Heart, and is but an emanation of God's soul. What is He but the sum of all things conceivable, in gentleness, in sweetness, in justice, in purity, in truth, in righteousness, in courage, in self-denial, in winningness, in heavenliness, in caress, in wisdom of philosophy, in beauty of poetry, in majesty of eloquence, and in magnitude of government? Whatever exercises the imagination worthily is possible to our conception, because it is in God. And can you keep the image all the time? It never should be the same, nor twice alike. It is forever changing, as the sky is forever changing—sometimes darkened with storms; sometimes covered with light, fleecy, floating, island-clouds; sometimes clear and tranquil, always varying, and yet always substantially the same. Our God changes not, in this: that He is holy, that He is blessed in love, that He is powerful in government, that He is drawing all creation toward Him, even as planets draw the tides of the sea toward them; and yet, after all, when you look at Him, so much is there of Him, so little can you take in of Him at once, that His attributes seem fugitive, and He does not seem to you twice alike. So great is He that there are no bounds to His greatness; so blessed is He that there are no terms that are adequate to describe Him; so unfailing is He that every heart says, "Thine, O God, am I, and Thou art mine".

※※※

God never revealed to man anything of moral or spiritual except through the foregoing experiences of men in regard to its moral quality. Whatever grows thus is the result of the application of the highest and the noblest truths to moral consciousness.

※※※

God's nature is not specialized and parceled out. God's great attributes are not like legal documents, written and sent by post to particular persons, none being allowed to take them out of the post-office except those whose names are on them. What God is, He is to all—or would be, if they would understand Him. The God of the whole earth is He. The universal Father is He. In Him there is neither Jew nor Gentile, bond nor free. All are as one in God.

※※※

The nature of God is the same to all men, but the effects are not the same on all men, because they do not all put it to the same uses. The reason why the sun produces in one place geraniums, camillias, azaleas, all forms of exquisite flowers, and does not produce them in another place, is not in the sun. The cause of the difference is in the use to which you put the sun. It shines on the south side of my barn; and what does it produce there? A warm spot, where chickens and cows gather. It shines on the south side of my neighbor's barn; and what does it produce there? Flowers and grapes. What is the reason of the difference? Does the sun change? No; but it is put to different uses. It is just the same sun, with just the same vivific power to all; but its effects are different when it is differently employed. In one man's hands it amounts to nothing, because he does not make any use of it; but in another man's hands it amounts to a great deal, because he does make use of it, and makes it do a great deal for him.

As to loving a God that is inconceivable, unthinkable, unknowable—it is preposterous. A morning-glory wants something that is solid to run up on. It wants to twine; but it will not twine on a shadow. It must have something that is substantial to twine on. Human nature, too, must have something substantial to twine on. And if you proclaim an immanent divinity, a kind of Soul-of-the-World, that has reason, though not anything that we understand by reason, that has justice, though not anything that we understand by justice, and that has goodness, though not anything that we understand by goodness, you will surely throw men into hopeless confusion! If when I say, "I love the truth", there is no correspondence between my sense of truth and truth as it exists in God, then the term "truth" is perpetually binding and enslaving me.

**

How beautiful art Thou, O Lord our God, that fillest our hearts with blessings, pourest the beautiful light day by day upon the earth, and floodest the heavens with Thy glory! And in all seasons of the year, Thine hand is still seen — Thine hand that creates beauty; that adorns strength with beauty. Thou throwest the robe thereof over the earth. Thy ways are wondrous. Thy paths drop fatness. Thou art known in the heavens, and Thou art known upon the earth, and yet Thou art unknown; and unsearchable art Thou. We see only Thine outward manifestations. The recesses of Thy love, the depths of Thy being, who can explore? Better art Thou than our best thoughts. More noble and beautiful art Thou than the highest imaginations of our most luminous hours. No mind hath thought Thee out. No tongue hath spoken Thee. No pen hath described Thee. Thine excellence cannot be measured. Thou art past finding out.

God is the heart and centre of the whole universe, and is lifting up men on His heart and carrying them in their weakness, planning for them, forbearing with them, solicitous of them, playing the universal father and the universal mother; suffering for men, not once in Gethsemane, not again on Calvary — these are simply types, specimens of that which has been going on — "the Lamb that was slain from the foundation of the world" — the Being that is most burdened, and the Being that suffers solicitude — not degrading suffering, not weakening suffering, but love suffering, that is full of gladness as well as suffering. For oftentimes it is the case that suffering is the sub-base of the organ underlying the grandeur of all the upper notes, and the beauty and the sweet tone of the instrument would be comparatively thin were it not that great undertone all the way through. And so it is with the nature of God.

* * *

My God is not one that looks out upon the universe with the short, hasty eye of time; He dwells in eternity. God has time enough for anything and everything. The revolving ages that seem to us endless in the past and endless in the future are as yesterday to God.

He is a fast workman; and I believe that when we shall come and appear in Zion the whole mighty problem of time will roll out, and in a perfect diapason of grandeur and love and joy, mankind will sing, "God is love and time benevolence".

* * *

How slowly do we understand Thee! How dark

are the simplest counsels of God to us! How often, in the night, do we cry out with the pangs of fear, because there is no answer to our yearnings! How often are we alone, and yet never alone! How often are we crushed under burdens which have beneath them, if we would, the power of omnipotence! How often do we attempt to stand, and fall when it is in our power to lean against Thee, so that nothing can overthrow us!

We know that Thou art to be found by those that humble themselves, and yet we refuse to go down, in our wisdom, and are forever building ourselves up in that pride which God cannot bless; and we are vagrants running to and fro, as if there had been no life before ours, no knowledge, no experience, no record of ways of righteousness, no faith of God, no government, and no providence. We care not. We shut our eyes and our ears, and go groping on to repeat the endless experiment of disaster. When shall the light pierce these dark eyes? When shall we have the simplicity of children, and believe in Thee? When shall we find our strength, our rest, our hope, and our life in God.

We have not come to Thee, our Father, simply because without Thee we perish. There is something that longs for Thee within us. There is the voice that will not be hushed. There is the soul that is sick without Thee, and that is homesick without assurance of heaven. There is the memory of all Thy past goodness. There is the memory of our own struggles upon which Thou didst place the victory. There is the memory of our defeats, and of our dungeon darkness which Thou didst visit. There is the memory of that peace which passeth all understanding, and which hath come to us. Even as the dove came and sat upon our Master, so upon us hath come the heavenly dove. As they that walk forth from winter toward the summer, and remember again all the things that are coming, and all the sweet smell of the field, and all the unrolling leaves, and all the fragrance of the quick-coming flowers that are before them, though they have been hidden long; so when we turn toward Thee from the winter and darkness of our earthly life, and we remember again what things have been; and Thou seemest to us most glorious, because of Thy goodness, Thy mercy, Thy gentleness, and Thy tenderness.

No man can learn his God out of a book. Out of nothing but his own experience can he learn it. Every man who has a God that is more than an empty name, has one that has been framed out of the actual conceptions and thoughts and feelings of his own nature. Little children fashion a God, sometimes full of fantasy, and sometimes full of sweet beauty; and it is their God, and all the God there is to them. Every man must take that which is in him, and for himself frame a name that is to him God. When you read in God's word, of justice, what you know of justice and what you think about justice will determine what that element is, as it enters into the framing of your God. If God be "holy and just and good", if He be "long suffering" and "plenteous in mercy", what do these names taken out of the sacred Scripture mean? To a bad man very little; to a good man, a great deal more; to a sainted man, still more. And if any man has a conception of God that touches his heart, and calls out his fervor and his self-denial, and makes him heroic, and fills him with joy, and with a wholesome sorrow, it is because he has the power given him to fashion a God that to him means something, in the same sense that his own experience means something.

If you do not know how to love, you cannot understand what love is in God. If you are bound hand and foot in utter selfishness, you cannot love a God that has magnanimity and disinterestedness. If you live for the flesh, you cannot exhale the sweet perfume of the spirit, as the fragrance of the flower rises above the form of the blossom. If you have no bright nature, how can you understand the ineffable, the spiritual, the infinite. By as much as God becomes possible and actual to you, by so much you have been transformed into that by which you now project, and by the imagination refine and give infinite proportions to — what you call your God.

As children away from home comfort themselves in the thought of father and mother, so we, while exiled from heaven, long to have the thought of Thee so near and so dear to us that we can run home in imagination, and be no more exiled, but ever present with the Lord.

* * *

We have a God that seeks men. You do not find Him, but He finds you. As a lamb is caught in the thorns and thickets, so men are caught in snares. And as one mired cannot go after relief, but must have relief come to him, so God searches for men that are snared. He goes out to find them. He is a Father. He is more than a Father — a God — for fatherhood is only one bright conception that sprang from the soul of God.

* * *

God clasps every soul that He once takes, and takes it for good or for bad. The wedding between the soul and God is one that knows no divorce, either here or hereafter.

* * *

Our God is not greater than we by the things in which He differs from us, so much as by His similarities to us. He is like us; but that likeness goes on augmenting. Love in God, for instance, is what love is in us; but that love which in us is but a throb, in Him augments to a volume inconceivable in our personality. Human nature, carried one way, runs toward the animal and the earthy. Carried in the other way, it runs toward spirit — toward God. The divine Being is not some mysterious and glorious other Being, but an infinite and inconceivably perfect manhood of the same sort as ours. When we see Him, we shall see Him as He is, and shall see ourselves more clearly in Him than we ever saw ourselves in ourselves.

God is the consummation of everything that is noble, beautiful and rare. Every quality that excites admiration in a generous or noble mind exists in God in infinite proportions and developments; and the growth which you have made is manifested by the receptivity which is in you when the name of God is disclosed. Not only is it "a name above every name", but it is a name that should bring to you thousands and thousands of the rarest and sweetest and noblest associations.

Oh, ye weary! why are you weary when others rest? Oh, ye sick! why do you suffer when others are healed? Oh, starving and hungering! there is bread enough. Oh, dying! there is life for you. Oh, desponding and despairing! look up and rejoice. A great light has arisen to those that sit in the region and shadow of death. Come to Christ who loves you, who is drawing you, and who has said to each one of you, "I will never leave thee nor forsake".

***

No man can have another man's Christ — if you will not misunderstand my words, and pervert my meaning. As a physician is who stands over you in sickness, so is Christ Jesus. What to your thought a teacher is who labors with you according to your ignorance, that is the Lord Jesus Christ. The prime consideration with every man is, "What is Christ to my soul?"

***

Be not Thou strange unto us, O Thou Saviour of our souls. Be present to our faith and to our secret apprehension. And then the rock will be soft; then the storm will be gentle; then sorrow itself will wing away. Be Thou present, Lord Jesus. There can be no trouble to the soul that rests in Thee. May we have this steadfast faith and this abiding hope; and at last may we be with Thee, which is better than life.

***

In the earlier period of Christian experience most men have a Christ that is extremely variable, not in the best sense of that term. It is a Christ of cloudy days, differing from the Christ of sunshiny days. It is the Christ of victorious hours, and a very different one from the Christ of Gethsemane. But little by little as we go on in life, we begin to find a unity in ourselves, so that at last the experiences that seem widely separate and scattered — all the elements of the dye-house, all the elements of the wool or the silk, all the elements of the loom, begin to come together, and are woven into one fabric, with a certain unity of design, in the loom of faith. And as we go on in life by faith in Christ Jesus our Lord, his brow grows broader, and the eye more benign, and the lips more sweet of love; and there comes to be that which does not change much, and the soul says, "I know in whom I have trusted." Although there may be evanescent changes here and there, we come to have a Christ that abides with us in all substantial elements. Then the soul rests, and says, "The Lord is my Shepherd, I shall not want". He leads us by the still waters and in green pastures. When we walk through the valley of the shadow of death, He is with us.

The truth remains the same, that every man's efficient Christ must have had such a relation to his personality and his history that in the most literal and intense sense of that term he can say, "Christ in me; my Christ". It cheats nobody. It takes Christ away from nobody. He belongs to me in many special respects; for nobody has had my struggles, nobody has had my temptations, nobody has had my deliverances, nobody has borne my griefs, but He and I together. Nobody has probed the darkness as I have; but He was my morning Star. Nobody has felt the cross, the yoke, and the burden that I have felt, or that you have felt each of you separately, individually and personally; and no one else can feel them except in my place, or in your place; and it is all these ministrations to you — the coming in mercy, the coming in judgment, the coming in reproof, the coming in encouragement and hope, or the coming in inexpressible love — that constitute Him to you something that He cannot be to anybody else.

It is the hope of my life, the longing of my life, to bring forth such a view of the character of God in Christ Jesus that every poor soul in the world shall be able to feel "He is mine, just as the sun is mine". And who owns the sun? The magnolia, beautiful, pure, with cups that diffuse incense to the very stars by night and the sun by day? Oh, yes; but not one whit more than the violet that grows near it. Who owns the sun? The bird that flies with brilliant plumage on every side? Certainly; but not one particle more than the barn-yard hen without a feather of beauty about her. Who owns the sun? The radiant beauties of the world? The toad, too. The sea is full of creatures that own the sun, and the air full of insects that own the sun, and the earth full of worms that own the sun, and everything that needs the sun owns it. And who needs God, and who owns God? Whoever wants Him; He is there for all. Whosoever will, let him come and take of God's swelling flood freely. It is not like an earthly substance that can be wasted by using it; it is the eternal existence of God's love. All those apparent contradictions and cacophonies that exist in human life, by and by, when the evil is removed, we shall see that there is a use in them; and, as in some of Beethoven's symphonies, there are passages that rasp the ear and that quiver the very foundations on which we stand, but are like gorges, which open out into valleys of beauty, made more beautiful by the contrast; so, by and by, in another life, we shall see that the things that in this life seemed such hard things were working out results that were beneficent and beautiful, past language.

Nothing is so exquisite in you, nothing is so multitudinous in you, nothing is so venomous and painful in you, in the way of moral temptations, that it has not had some part in the experience of Christ, so that it is interpreted to Him perfectly. And every sigh, every groan, every aspiration, every thought, that will not even look up, but that, looking down, despairs—God knows them all, and knows them quick; for they bound, as it were, against His heart, bringing up suggestions of trials in His own self.

There is no experience among us that goes far, compared to the distance and route it travels, when judged by the Divine and the Infinite. The chord in our souls is short and stubborn. The chord in the Divine soul is infinite; and its vibrations are immeasurably beyond any experience of our own. Sorrow in us is of the same kind as sorrow in God; and yet, as compared with the sorrow of God, human sorrow is but a mere puff. Love moves in no such circles as it does in God. In Him it is never dimmed by any such glooms of fear, nor sullied by any such smoke of passions, as it is in us. It is not in Jesus, as in us, a mere household taper, burning when sheltered, and at that throwing its light less and less strongly the more the space is augmented. God is a sun, and His love goes out like sunlight, infinite, inexhaustible, not measured like a vintner's cup, to a precise quantity, but, without measure, overflowing as the waters; unfathomable as the ocean; all persuasive as the light and the heat.

***

Jesus Christ's heart is the nest of the soul. Scared by any trouble, by any disappointment, by any sorrow, pursued as birds by hawks, there is a refuge. There He will give you rest. "Take my yoke upon you, and my burden, and you shall find rest unto your souls. My yoke is easy, my burden is light." Whoever puts himself in agreement with the heart, thought and feeling of God as manifested in Jesus Christ, has, in all his sorrow and trouble, a refuge in the Saviour which never fails. The greater the darkness the clearer the light; the greater the assault the surer the defence; the greater the sorrow the greater the rest. The heart which knows how to put itself into the trust and love of the Lord Jesus Christ is not released from suffering; but it nevertheless can say, with the psalmist, "God hath dealt bountifully with me; return unto thy rest, O my soul!"

**

Our strength is in God; our comfort is in Him; but He must be a God that the broken-hearted and the consciously imperfect can walk with without being driven by fear, or kept under the pressure of perpetual shame. That God is revealed in Jesus Christ.

**

I would not say that God turns the brightest side of His nature to those who have stumbled and fallen, but in all those ways in which men are harassed by condemning conscience, by a sense of mistake that might have been avoided; in all their struggles under great sorrows and bereavements; in all those sorrows which tug at life like the racking teeth of a double saw; in those sorrows which come in a rain of distress; in all the alarms of life, in all the seductions of business, in all the burdens that come upon men — over against them stands a Saviour adapted to the special sorrow that they themselves carry. He is all in all; that is, in every part of a man's life, and in every special trouble there is an aspect of God in Jesus Christ that mitigates the special trouble, that is adapted to the special want; and the revelation of God's love in Jesus

Christ is a revelation that should enable every man who puts trust in Him, and accepts Him as the Guide and Captain of his salvation, to rise higher. It lifts him in the time of his emergency, shelters him in danger, guides him in his bewilderments and his perplexities, and brings him to that rest which does not depend upon conscious purity, but depends upon a sense of God's love, and upon trust and faith in Him.

Have you any Christ? No two conceptions of Christ are alike. It is vain for you to look over to this one and that one. Have you any Christ that carries your characteristics in it? Have you a biography that He expresses to your memory or thought? Has He been to you a Revealer, a Sustainer and a Helper in time of need?

Have you ever laid your head, as John did, on the bosom of your Saviour? Perhaps you have striven after Madame Guyon's Christ, or after the Christ of Augustine, or after the Christ that Wesley found, or after the Christ of some minister who has helped you, or after the Christ of some mother, sister, wife, or friend; but every man's Christ must come out of his own soul.

Is Christ in us — in every one of us? Something of His cradle and His poverty; something of the youth and the toil of the young Jesus; something of the conflicts and the beggary of His life; something of His bitter trial; something of His Gethsemane and something of His death—out of these has your Christ sprung?

"I am the way," said Christ, as if He had laid Himself down along the rocky, flint-cutting road, and said to men, "Walk on me, I am your road". And the whole spirit and temper of the Scriptures is on behalf of those that are low down, to lift them up.

The vision of Christ that comes to you through your personal experience is higher than the judgment of any philosophy; higher than any result that you can make by analysis or by recomposition—by synthesis. When out of your soul-needs, and the revelation of your soul-experiences, you find before you the constant picture of this thought, and the joy of your soul, do not undertake to repaint it by the reason. Let it float before you in all its beautiful hues, and in all its pristine forms. Let your Christ be the disembodied Christ of the imagination, bearing to your various necessities patience, or gentleness, or courage, or joy, or hope, which you shall see reflected from His benign face.

A man is privileged to have a Christ that seems to

him to have been born out of the elements of necessity in him. It is "Christ in you, the hope of glory", formed out of your necessities, out of your yearnings, out of your aspirations, out of your sorrows, out of your joys, out of your temptations. It is the Christ that has been around about you through the series of your days and years, over against every facet of the diamond soul; so that your individuality is inseparably wrapped up with your conception of the Jesus that is yours. It may be less glorious than another's, or it may be more glorious than another's; but it is yours. It is Christ as seen through your soul's inspection, and as revealed to you by all the spiritual and temporal necessities of your history and your life. It is born in you an infant, growing up in you, as it were, through its youth; that is, your youth of knowledge, becoming regent, and at last triumphant in you, so that you can say, "Whom have I in heaven but Thee? There is none on earth that I desire beside Thee."

There was not in Jesus Christ one single power that throbs and vibrates in the human soul that was not tried beyond anything that we are ever tried with in this mortal life.

Christ's mission was to reconcile men to God — not to reconcile God to men. He came to bring out a power which should cause men to lift their eyes and see that whatever was romantic in love on earth, that whatever was faithful in affection in the household, that whatever sacrifice there was in love, that whatever there was of kindness and mercy, was the interior nature of God. There stands the Sun of Righteousness, blazing with this one radiant interpretation: that God so loved the world that He gave His only begotten Son to die for it.

One drop of Christ's blood is worth more than the round globe, though it were one orbicular diamond; and souls are God's jewels.

If I lose everything else, I will stand on the sovereign idea that God so loved the world that He gave His own Son to die for it rather than it should die. To tell me that back of Christ there is a God who for unnumbered centuries has gone on creating men and sweeping them like dead flies — nay, like living ones — into hell, is to ask me to worship a being as much worse than the conception of any mediæval devil as can be imagined; but I will not worship the devil, though he should come dressed in royal robes and sit on the throne of Jehovah. I will not worship cruelty. I will worship Love — that sacrifices itself for the good of those that err, and that is as patient with them as a mother is with a sick child. With every power of my being will I worship as God such a being as that.

* * *

Do you ask me if I believe in the atonement of Christ. I believe in the atonement of God. I believe that there is no other atonement but that everlasting nature of God which spares the weak, which pardons the guilty, which draws men out of themselves, which is long-suffering, but which says, "There shall forever be a difference between truth and lies, between right and wrong"; which says, "Forever and forever selfishness shall be painful, and benevolence shall be blessed; and I will maintain that which is high and noble, and will bring the race up to it by stripes, by chastisements, by tears, by suffering, by long trial; and I will bear and forbear with them, never forgetting that I am striving for the glorious enfranchisement of the animal into manhood, and for the elevation of manhood into the sonship of God; and I will see that men shall not be contented and untroubled in wrong ways. I will smite and punish; but the smiting and the punishing will be for the sake of making my love manifest. Whom I love I chasten, and I scourge every son that I receive."

* * *

The whole earth would have dwindled and gone out if it was not for one glowing spot — Calvary. For that mountain it shall stand forever and glowing through all space, shine as a mighty Jewel that God hath set as a memorial of His everlasting love.

God so loved the world that he gave his Son to die for it. There was no such palliation or placation needed in the Divine disposition as required any sacrifice of Christ Jesus. If the revelation of God himself in the mercy, in the wisdom, in the purity, in the truth, in the love of Jesus Christ; if the life and sufferings and death of Jesus Christ wrought out such a view of God as to make His goodness, His grandeur, and His glory more apparent to the comprehension of men, and so more attractive than it was before—that is reason enough for the coming of Jesus Christ, that is atonement enough. Any view of the Divine nature that makes Him first angry, and then placated, is blasphemous. God's brooding love, not God's irritable law, is the doctrine of the Bible. God avenging is not the doctrine of the Bible. God loving and saving is the doctrine of the Bible.

It is time, I think, that we should say not that we are saved by the blood of Christ, but that the blood of Christ represents the love and devotedness of Christ, by whose sufferings we are saved. Is not Divine sympathy more potent upon men's thoughts than blood? Are we forever to be saturating the popular imagination with this physical symbol which was meant to carry us up to spiritual ideas? Are we to abandon the spiritual idea, and go back to the barbarity and captivity of the external and the physical form of the symbol? I believe that we are saved by the blood of Christ, because I believe the blood of Christ signifies His love. It is an expression to show the utmost fidelity and love, and willingness of suffering in love, for the moral inspiration and redemption of mankind.

* *
*

As the Interpreter of God's great love, as the means of opening to our understanding what is the atoning power of God's heart and disposition, Jesus Christ came into this world; and it behooved Him to be like unto His brethren; and he accepted the necessity. It behooved Him to be a man of sorrows, and acquainted with grief, because all great men who have given themselves for the good of the world have been men of sorrows and acquainted with grief. Groans have echoed since the world began, and will echo till the end of time. Lamentations, sorrows in every form, prevailed from the first, and were to prevail until the last; and it behooved Christ to be like unto His brethren. He joined Himself to the human family, and lived, and died, and rose again; and, dying and living for us, as our Instructor, as our Exemplar, as our Leader, as the Pacifier of rebellious human nature, and as the Interpreter, by His life, by His teaching, by His death, of the reconciliation of men to God, He has a claim upon every human soul to whom the knowledge comes. None of us have a right to live to ourselves, but all of us are under obligation to live to Him who redeemed us by His precious blood.

* * *

God is so infinite, and in quality so exquisite, that He could only be known by a representation of Himself, and He took out from the bosom of His love His Son Jesus.

* * *

O throne of iron, from which have been launched terrible lightnings and thunders that have daunted men! O throne of crystal, that has coldly thrown out beams upon the intellect of mankind! O throne of mystery, around about which have been clouds and darkness! O throne of Grace, where He sits regnant Who was my brother, Who has tasted of my lot, Who knows my trouble, my sorrow, my yearning and longing for immortality! O Jesus, crowned, not for Thine own glory, but with power of love for the emancipation of all struggling spirits! Thou art my God — my God!

* * *

Above our father and our mother, above our children and our companions, above our truest friends, there rises the face divine of Jesus, our Lord, our soul's Saviour, Who found us, and taught us to find Him; Who loves us with an unfathomable love; Who gave Himself for us; and Who redeemed us from death, from sin, and from all impurity, that He might make us His own, waiting for us, our Mediator, our Intercessor, our Forerunner. All that the soul needs in its mission in this life, and its mortal march, Thou doest, O Lord, our Saviour, for us.

**

Jesus Christ came to make known to the human race, in tones that will vibrate to the last centuries of time, the central truth that God is supreme and sovereign, not because He is perfect, and not because He is lifted above care and trouble, but because He has in Him a heart and soul that feels for sin, for infirmities, for sorrows, for mistakes; for all that goes to wreck and ruin. Such was the Divine nature, brought to us in a language which we can understand, through the incarnation of the divine Spirit in Jesus Christ, and revealing to us, not something gotten up as an episode, not something interjected upon the course of time, but that God was the eternal Father of ages, and that He was a Being whose sympathies were vital, universal, exquisite, and full of stimulating, rescuing power. And for the ages and ages yet to come, the eternal sovereign is to be named Father; and He earns and deserves the title, by having transcendently and infinitely more compassion and sympathy and suffering power for those who are in peril than any earthly parent has.

**

I have been asked, "Do you believe in the Atonement?" Which? I believe in mine; I believe that my God has made known to me in Jesus Christ His atonement for the sins of the world, and that it inheres in the Divine nature and overpours and fills time, and will fill all eternity. I believe that but for this redeeming love of God in Jesus Christ no man would ever rise higher than the vegetable or the animal, and that it is the inspiration of the world. He impletes the heart, the soul with Himself, and He is all in all. I believe in Jesus Christ — that is the whole thing.

O Lord, forgive our want of trust, and clothe us in the spirit of childlike faith and confidence. May all Thy words seem to us Yea and Amen! And we pray that Thou wilt grant that in time to come we may dwell more by the power of faith. With Thee above the cloud — above the storm — above the reach of the fowler, and of his arrow — there, under the shadow of Thy wings, may we find perfect peace.

Faith that can be unsettled by the access of light and knowledge had better be unsettled.

It is faith that does things in this world. When men pray, believing, their prayers are effectual. The fact is, praying is very much like chestnut-gathering among boys. They go out with their little clubs, and throw them into the trees, but the chestnuts do not fall, and they go away thinking there are none; but the frost in the night loosens them, and they come rattling down upon the ground, and the boys wonder where they came from. They were in the trees all the time, but they did not reach them with their little clubs. You have got to throw high enough and strong enough, and then the results will come rattling down. Men, for the things which they solicit at the hand of God, throw little prayers, and do not throw them above their heads, and oftentimes not as high as that; and then they get together and wonder if prayers of faith are of any consequence, and question whether there is any such thing as a prayer of faith.

***

Faith in the Lord Jesus Christ is not any mythical state; it is the enthusiasm of a follower who reveres his leader. It is the rapture of one who looks up confidingly toward a beloved master. It is the personal effluence of a soul toward Christ under the consciousness of its relationship to Him.

***

God says, "Here is your duty for to-day, and the means with which to do it. To-morrow you will find remittances and further directions; next week you will find other remittances and other directions; next month you will find others; and next year still others."

* * *

There is no place where God puts you, where it is not your duty to turn round, and say, "How shall I perfume this place, and make it fragrant as the honeysuckle and the violet, and beautiful as the rose?" In this world you are to perform the great duties of spiritual, moral and physical life in the place where you are.

* * *

If you go out in the fields, and should want to gather nettles, take care how you handle them; if you grasp them firmly they will not hurt you, but touch them lightly, and you will find your hands stung all over. Just so with duty; grasp it hard and the sting is gone.

* * *

If your work be mean or disagreeable, let your religion weave over it a network of flowers, beautify it with piety, but never desert it; that sacrifice is more acceptable to your God than incense and burnt-offering.

* * *

Every duty, however mean, should be the altar on which you place your offering to God; all your daily labors should be as acts of devotion, and so your life would become one entire consecration.

What if the path be thorny; it is but a little while. What if the flints do cut; it is but a short passage.

Providence never puts a man on any path of duty without making provision for his safety.

Duties which were harsh and acrid at the first, if boldly undertaken and consistently borne, become ruddy to the eye, fragrant to the smell, sweet to the taste. Duty carries the wine of strength and inspiration within itself.

He that is false to present duty, breaks one thread in the great fabric; sometime the plan will be found. Then he may have forgotten the breaking of the thread and imagine that troubles spring out of the ground.

If God makes saints of any of us he will have to put us in the very lowest class to begin. No one can be a candidate for saintship unless he is willing cheerfully to perform the duties that fall to his lot in the place where he is. When he has completely filled that place the call will assuredly be heard, "Come up higher". We must rise as a seed rises. The acorn is quite content to be only an acorn, it is content to go out of sight, and hide its roots where no eye can see. If you want eminent experiences, be willing to begin at the lowest room.

There is no avoirdupois in duty. When duties are powerfully attracted by the willing soul within, they have no weight.

Christ identifies Himself with the weakness, and the bitterest trials of life, and the performance of duties in these places is a flower of remembrance pressed in the book of life, never to be lost. Go through the garden of your life and see what flowers you can present to God. If you have the fairest and most exquisite blossoms, gather and present them; they will be graciously accepted. If you have them not, then take the best you have, though coarse. God will not reject nor throw them out. If you have not even garden flowers, go and seek chickweed and little humble dust-covered blossoms by the wayside. God will take them since they are the best you have. But go search again, if you cannot find even wayside weeds, are you willing to thrust your hand into the thorn bush and among nettles, for the sake of making a present to Christ — and go to Him and say, "Lord Jesus, I have but these". He will look on the wounded, lacerated hand, and He that wore the crown of thorns for you will take the gift and press it to His bosom, saying, "My child, you did this for my sake; the love they manifest makes them sweeter far than most beautiful flowers".

Christ incarnates Himself again for every one of us in those duties which are most painful or irksome for us to perform, that, instead of a motive derived from the work itself, we may do it as unto Him.

Sinai may smoke; but let Calvary sigh and say, "Father", and Calvary is the mightier of the two.

You might, by the north wind, throw the convolvulus, the morning-glory, the queen of flowers, prostrate along the ground; but it is only when the warm sun gives it leave that it twines upward about that which is to support it, and blesses it a thousand fold by its efflorescence all day long. The terrors of the Lord may dissuade men from evil; but it is the warm shining of the heart of God that brings men toward His goodness and toward Him.

Fear never works through the inward nature to goodness, but upon the outward in conduct. It may produce a dread of wrong, but never a yearning for right.

Do not think you do God honor when you go, bowed down in fear and trembling, before Him. He seems to say, "Why, why, with averted face do you treat me as if I were your master? I have nothing in the universe to which you are not heir—joint heir with Christ, your elder brother." That one word, "Father", transfers everything to your possession.

Religion is harmonious human nature. It includes every element which manhood includes. It is wholesomeness of soul. It is manhood on a higher plane.

Many persons have an idea that religion is a policy of insurance against future fire, and if once they have paid in, why, that has settled it, and it will stand.

Religion is character, it is permanence in a man's

own nature, it is a new life, it is being born again and built up on a higher plane; and when a man has just enough education to be fretting because he has no more, just enough to keep awake in him his conscience, his fears, his dreads, I will not say he had better have none, but I will say that he does not know nor can he know what the full fruition of God's Spirit in the human soul is, for if religion is worth anything it is worth everything.

* * *

Natural religion is generally considered as poor stuff. Imported is thought more of than home-made —broadcloth proves better than linsey-woolsey. The church thinks that it will not do to make religion too easy; folks might take it up of themselves.

* * *

Secret religion is good and necessary; secreted religion is mean.

* * *

Religion is simply right living. In both Old and New Testaments it is called Righteousness. It begins as a seed. It develops as a growth. It is relative to the individual characteristics, to the age, the institutions, the whole economy of life.

Your true religious life consists in standing where God has put you, and exercising Christian qualities. It consists in showing pity where pity is called for; in manifesting patience where patience is required; in exhibiting gentleness where gentleness is needed. It consists in forbearing with others; in bearing others' burdens; in not being easily provoked; in thinking no evil, when evil things are brought to you; in loving where other men would hate; in doing where others would sit still. In other words, as it is indispensable that the mathematician should make an application of his problem, so it is necessary that the theory of religion should be applied to life.

No man has more religion than he lives.

Creeds are not religion; philosophy is not religion; knowledge is not religion. The right conduct of a man in his physical life is a part of it; his right conduct in social relations is another part of it; his right conduct in relation to God and the spiritual future, is another and higher part of it; and a man has just so much religion as he is enabled to develop in all these different relations of his mortal life.

Men use religion just as they use buoys and life-preservers; they do not intend to navigate the vessel with them, but they keep just enough of them on hand to float into a safe harbor when the storm comes up, and the vessel is shipwrecked; and it is only then that they intend to use them. I tell you, you will find airholes in all such life-preservers as that.

Religion is the building of a manhood upon the model of Jesus Christ. It is not doing this, or doing that. It is attempting to set up in ourselves the kingdom of heaven, which is said to be within us. It is not a thing, a proportion, a quality, a force, but manhood, man-building — that is the very genius of the Gospel.

The old theology is from the forge, from law, from government among men; the New Testament theology takes its centre in the Fatherhood of God and in the Divine Love.

True religion is like fruit; when the sun has turned the acid juices of it to sweetness, the fruit is delicious; but in the early season it is not — it is sour and bitter. There are thousands of Christian men and women that are perpetually eating green fruit.

***

Many a man's religion is like his Sunday clothes, which he takes out of the closet very carefully on Sunday morning, puts them on, brushes them all down, and looks at himself in the glass, and feels as though he was presentable; and in his Sunday clothes he goes to church, and he sings — oh, how loud! And he prays or he groans — oh, how audibly! And he has a very pleasant ear for music, and the sermon pleases him, and he goes home saying, "How beautiful is religion!" On Monday he takes off the coat and hangs it up again, and all the other articles, and puts on his worldly clothes, and goes about his business. Now, religion is no garment to be changed; it is a state of the soul. It may begin little, but it grows, and no man can lay it aside, no man can supersede it by anything else. It is education; it is the reconstruction of a man's inward life and nature upon a nobler pattern than any that Nature can give us; and there is no such thing as putting it on for this, and taking it off for that. It is character. Reputation may change, character does not easily; and the habits of the soul formed upon everlasting truth and Divine influence — that is religion, and it does not come in a day, it does not come in the flesh.

The true religious man is a man who is positive and affirmative. A man who has nothing more than *nots*, is nothing. To be anything, he must have actual virtues.

* * *

There are a great many people who think that religion means not doing wrong. As if a knitting machine would be considered good, that never knit any stockings, because it never misknit! What is a man good for who simply does *not* do some things?

* * *

Religion is not love to God alone; it is love to man as well.

* * *

Ye, who mourn because particular modes are changing, and think that religion is dying out, look deeper and pluck up hope out of your despair, and confidence out of your fear. And you who think religion is going away because of science, let me say that science is the handmaid of religion; it is the John the Baptist oftentimes, that clears the way for true religion. By religion I do not mean outward things but inward states. I mean perfected manhood. I mean the quickening of the soul by the beautific influence of the Divine Spirit in truth, and love, and sympathy, and confidence, and trust. That is not dying out. Not until the soul of man is quenched can religion die out. Not until God ceases to be God can religion be quenched in this world. It may have its nights and days; it may have its winter and summer; it may be subject to the great laws of oscillation and change; but, nevertheless, the word of God standeth sure; its foundations are immutable; and not until the last tear has been shed, not until the last pulse of love has throbbed, not until the new heavens and the new earth appear, will religion die on earth or lose its power among men.

All the elements of manhood, in their right place and action, are constituent parts of religion; but no one of them alone is religion. It takes the whole manhood, imbued and inspired of God, moving right both heavenward and earthward, to constitute religion.

He who is using his whole self according to laws of God, is religious. Some men think devotion is religion. Yes, devotion is religion; but it is not all of religion. Here is a tune written in six parts; and men are wrangling and quarreling about it. One says that the harmony is in the bass; another, that it is in the soprano; another, that it is the tenor, and another that it is in the alto; but I say that it is in all the six parts. Each may, in and of itself, be better than nothing; but it requires the whole six parts to make what was meant by the musical composer. Some men say that love is religion. Well, love is, certainly, the highest element of it; but it is not that alone. Justice is religion; fidelity is religion; hope is religion; faith is religion; obedience is religion. These are all part and parcel of religion. Religion is as much as the total of manhood; and it takes in every element of it.

***

I believe God is giving new birth to us as He is to all Nature all the time, and that it is the result of Divine will, but not in the mechanical way, not with that irresistibleness. I believe it is the result of the Divine will, just as heat in the sun is the irresistible cause of moss and grass, and flowers, and shrubs, of grapes and fruit of every kind. No tree can stand up and say, "I made myself a pippin". He is not going to nod his proud head as if he did it himself. He had the element in him out of which the tree came, and the fruit came; but all came from the sun, and if there had been an eclipse, he never would have sprouted, let alone become the father of fruit; and I believe no man in life ever thinks, wills, or has any upward aspiration, or any longings, any soul life, that God is not the author of. "In Him we live and move and have our being."

To the spiritual man, the higher manhood, the man of the spirit, and not of the flesh; all the impulses of his life, everything that he has, "By the grace of God I am what I am". It is the circumambient influence, the universal, immanent God, the God everywhere and always, and in all things; that is the pabulum of life, is the spiritual stimulus by which we do anything that is higher than animal life itself.

As the sun shining upon the trees is felt by the roots that are buried deep in the earth, and that never see the light which brings forth from them, that which is the nourishment of the whole tree, and that produces the bud, and the leaf, and the blossom that cover it; so great, that the shining of Thy face upon us may reach down to the deepest parts of our nature, and that every element of our life may be so penetrated with Thine influence that we may bear fruit to Thine honor and glory.

Men are like prisoners in a dungeon, and God, like a harper, plays sweet melodies beneath their prison walls, if so be he may arouse a thought of home within them; but if they begin to be moved by the familiar sounds, pride and passion, their stern jailers try to shut them down in deeper dungeons, where no sound shall reach them.

While you want no consolation, while there is music enough in the world for you, you feel no want of God. When you long for God in conscious poverty and misery, feeling that you cannot live without Him, be sure that you shall find Him. He will throw around you the arm of His influence — then you shall know these hidden truths which the world cannot perceive.

***

The highest proof of any truth is moral consciousness. When a soul is conscious of being carried beyond itself in light, and peace, and joy, it has absolute proof that it is under the power of God's spirit. This may not be proof to other minds. That will depend upon the condition of those minds. A bell when struck will awaken vibrations in other bells, if they are keyed to the same tone.

***

Shabby as a beggar is, he is better off than if he was stark naked on a cold winter day. Though your morality is inferior, it is a world better off than to have nothing at all. But how glorious is that clothing of the Spirit that God gives to those that ask Him in faith and in humility!

As the touch of a musician brings differing sounds from the different strings of a harp, so the Divine touch, or inbreathing on the soul, brings forth results according to the individual nature of each person. But the variety, volume, combinations, intensities of the Divine influence upon the souls of different persons is a theme not yet explored and reduced to knowledge.

Jesus taught that the mind, opened and stimulated by the Divine soul, could bring forth emotions, dispositions, moral intuitions, joys, and visions such as do not come out of mere morality, nor out of ordinary influences in secular life. It was as if He had said, "You know no more about what you are, undeveloped in the higher possibilities, than a man knows what the seed is, that stops before it blossoms".

The Spirit of God is that Spirit by which universal growth takes place; and there is the power of God given forth to every soul that wants it, and opens itself to it, to be regenerated by the power of the Holy Ghost. It is not a hard command that we should not be converted in any other way than that; it is a most gracious permission, it is a glorious annunciation. In your struggle upward God is on your side, working out your own salvation with fear and trembling, for it is God that is working in you to will and to do of His good pleasure.

Glory be to God that a man may be converted, and that he has Divine help!

* * *

The true life in this world is the life that is going on in the soul of man. No man knows what he is until he has risen beyond the height of literature and social pleasure. No man knows what the soul is capable of being, or feeling, what vast circuits it can make, what voluminous experiences it can have, what strange triumphs belong to it, or what endurances and victories it can achieve, until he is brought under the influence of God.

This is true soul feeding—feeding the soul by staining it through with God's love, dropping gently upon it, as the darkest thunder-clouds are stained through by roseate hues of light, and turned to glory; the coming down upon the soul of Divine enthusiasms which throw their fiery sparks all through it, and kindle it with light and life and power; the coming of the influence of God's nature to the soul, brooding it, striking through it, rousing it up.

When one comes under the conscious influence of the Divine Spirit, the soul lifts itself up with unwonted clearness, faith, joy, trust, effluence and liberty. What a bird was when it lay in its little round nest, an egg, compared with what it is when it sings in the dewy morning, near heaven's gate—that is the soul in the body compared with what it is in the joy of sweet and loving intercourse with God through Jesus Christ our Lord.

* *

O, what a tranquil sea that is when a man can cast anchor in the heart of Jesus! What wind can greatly disturb him?

* *

When men come under the Divine influence, their life is said to be hid. Yes, it is hid; not simply eclipsed as it is in sleep, but hid by rising so much higher than the lower life, that the lower life does not interpret it fairly. It has gone out of sight. Only in that sense is it hid.

* *

It is a life which comes to some by flashes. It is a life which comes to some by blessed dreams. There is a kind of spiritual haze which seems to befall some men, as there is an Indian summer which befalls the year; but there is also a true life. It is possible for the human soul to live in abundance and freedom and blessedness, so that it shall be forever at rest and at peace.

* *

Soul knows how to interpret soul. I do not want any one to tell me that a person is patient if I live with him. I do not want any one to teach me that a person is genial and gentle if I live with him. I see it. It informs the feature, it inspires the action, or it represses activity. I know it without words and without analysis. And if this be true in the lower ranges of experience, how much more is it true in the very highest, where the soul from day to day is brooded by the Spirit of Almighty God and dwells in the imperial consciousness! Because He lives I live; I live in Him; He in me; God in Christ, Christ in God; I at one with Christ, as He is with God — this is the mystic language of that higher consciousness. It is profound and elusive, but it is real and glorious.

Mere philosophy will never interpret God to us. Some of His works it will interpret, but not Him. He is a spirit; and only a spirit can understand Him, only that spirit which is of Him and in Him can interpret the ever-present God. It is only through the intuitions of our dispositions, rarefied, scantified, opened, impleted with the Divine Nature, that we can bring God near.

I think if there is any one thing that has been misinterpreted, it is the doctrine of the Divine influence upon the human soul. As I recollect my own belief as a child — and I was an orthodox child — I believed that when a man who was born a sinner, and who had grown up in sin, came to a certain age, and went through a proper fermentation, and had dejected the lees, as it were, and left the wine of life pretty clear above, he was converted. I believed that he then passed from the north side of the hedge, where it was shady, to the south side, where the sun always shone. I believed that God shone on His elect, that they had the Divine influence, and that no others had. But my impression now is, that there is not a single human soul that is not the product of the Divine Spirit, and that that Spirit is the vivific element of the universe; and that as the sun in spring knocks at the tomb of every sleeping plant, and there is a resurrection wherever there is a bud or germ, and there is not a daisy, or harebell, or ranunclus, or flower of any kind that does not start at the solicitation of the sun's light and warmth; so the roots of power being here in human souls, there must be a shining of the Divine Soul directly upon them to bring out in them intelligence, emotions and moral sentiments. This down-shining of God is universal.

Mountains hold commerce with God's invisible ocean in the air, as good men endure by intercourse with the Invisible. Even in the droughts of summer, mountain streams are full-pulsed when all else is parched with fever.

Truth is food, and is to be fed as men can bear it.

All truth in the beginning is very much like gold at

first. There is more rock than gold, and it is only after it has been stamped and ground to powder, and has gone through the chemical bath, that the gold is separated from the dross.

When truth in any age has apparently been destroyed, it has only died as the seed dies, to come up again a hundred-fold. He that smites the thistle, replants the thistle over broad places. He that smites the ripe barley head and the ripe wheat is a sower of the seed, though he may destroy the seed-bed in which it ripens. The apparent destruction of influences for good, buries them only that they may come up again. The persecuting of them is only that they may be scattered everywhere. How the thrashing-floor contrasts with the sowing of the seed! The tender nature of the one process, the violence of the other! Yet the flail separates wheat from straw and chaff.

The truths a man preaches ought to be to him like household words, and even to drop an inferior truth for a superior one ought to be to him like taking leave of a friend.

Men are like cathedral windows, kaleidoscopic with stained glass of all manner of colors and shades, each piece transmitting light of its own peculiar color; and the revelation of truth is according to the faculties in the men themselves through which it reports itself.

* * *

All night long the snow charges down without clash or sound of trumpet. In the morning, fence and forest, hedge and herb and the low-growing grasses all over the field are covered by it. Is that the sign of summer? Is this flocculent descent, that lies upon the white bosom of the field in all the region round about, a token of a harvest? Harvest out of snow? Yes; for it broods softly upon the earth, and keeps it warm. It is indeed a good thing for all the hidden roots that are waiting to grow and develop. And as the sun sails northward, and the days and nights grow warmer, it changes its form and flies away, some of it to the air to keep the sponge moist yet, and some of it downward, carrying not alone itself. As the air is filled with gases everywhere, that have ascended from decaying vegetation and from human habitations, ammoniacal vapors, the snow catches them and carries them down, and has come thus to have the name of the poor man's manure. So, as it melts, it distributes through all the ground its health-giving, restoring and reviving properties. By and by the shoots of grass begin to come, and the early flowers come, and along in the spring, especially in the further northern regions where there is but a short summer, things make haste to jump and grow, and these are the children of the snow. It came as death comes; its appearance was that of a shroud, but it bore in its bosom a silent life—a life not unfolded. It gave itself to the earth, and when by and by in vapors, little by little, it comes up again to hang as beautiful clouds in the summer—hang throughout all these regions, it has not returned unto God void. It has gone as a missionary goes, and has borne its message of life and growth to all the fields, and has accomplished that whereunto it was sent.

"So shall my word be," saith God.

Truth never enters the world as an army, a thousand men abreast. Truth always comes as John the Baptist came, in the wilderness, clothed in camel's hair, and for the most part eating locusts and wild honey. It cannot get anything better.

If you suppose that when God, Who knows all things in their infinite relations, rather than in their limited time relations, Who sees the end from the beginning, Who lives in a largeness of which we have no conception, Who is in a sphere removed infinitely further from us than we are from the beetle that burrows under the bark—if you suppose that when He attempts to teach men, who are shut up to matter, inclosed in the flesh, He will address them from His own standpoint, you have no true conception of the Divine procedure. His standpoint of truth is one, and ours is another; and we must judge by that which is taught us in our circumscribed sphere, in the realm of our limited knowledge, while He judges by His boundless knowledge in a sphere which is no less in extent than the universe itself. Though it may be compatible for us to have the beginnings of an understanding of the Divine nature, it is impossible for us to have such a conception of it as God Himself has. The difference between a pure spirit in the spiritual realm and a soul in the body, surrounded by immutable physical laws, is one which leads to endless mistakes, unless we are willing to accept rudimentary, alphabetic ideas with humility.

* * *

Great truths, like great cannon, are often left lying in the dust because they are so great that men cannot easily use them, and their recoil is proportioned to their power.

* * *

Every truth has to go through its martyr period of trial, darkness and crucifixion, and men must go with it, and not till it emerges from the grave does it appear in glory and victory. This was the experience of the holy men of old, and this is the experience of all who do any great good for their times. Victory may be delayed, yet the spirit of justice, of benevolence, of liberty may be gaining ground. Our business is not to date God's victories, but to prepare the way for them.

* * *

No man can express the great truths of human life without employing all his moral and æsthetic nature. No man ever delivers great truths worthily without rising into eloquence and even into poetry.

* * *

A creed is just like a philosopher's telescope. He sweeps the heavens to see if he can find the star for which he is searching; and by and by the glass brings it to his eye. The glass helps him; but it is not the glass that sees the star. It is the eye that does that. The glass is a mere instrument by which to identify the star, and magnify it, and bring it near, and shut off other things. A blind man could not see a heavenly body with a telescope by which we identify philosophical truths, and magnify them, and bring them near; but it is the heart that is to apprehend them. It is the heart that is to interpret the things that are marked out by our creed or philosophy.

* * *

Jerusalem is pictured in the Revelations as having twelve gates. Of course the idea came from the twelve tribes of Israel and the twelve patriarchs (not one of whom, I should think, got into heaven, though, by the way they acted); but one thing is very certain, that if a city has got twelve gates, the men that cannot go in at one gate, can go in at another and opposite one, and they have to take different roads to get into them.

Now, if a man wishes to go to Chicago, and wishes to go by the way of Alabama, it is perfectly permissible; it will take him longer and cost him more, and fatigue him more, but when he has come to Chicago he has got there just as much as if he had gone in a straight line.

So, in regard to the great things of religion, and love to God and love to man, if once they reach that! One man can do it through the Catholic church; in God's name let him do it—I don't care how far he travels, if he gets there. Another man can do it in the silence of the Quaker church; let him, that is his lookout, not mine, only get there. Another man goes through Presbyterianism, Westminster Catechism and all; the whole creation groans and travails in pain until now, if he goes that way, nevertheless it is his liberty, only so he gets there. The heavenly city has twelve gates, and there must be at least twelve different paths to get there.

I am not for undenominationalising men. I believe in sects. I believe that the Baptists ought to be Baptists simply because they think so, and as a man thinketh so he is. I think that the Calvinist that is genuinely misled into that, ought to stand by his guns. I think that the Presbyterian Church ought to be Presbyterian, and the Methodist Church ought to be Methodist, and the Episcopal Church ought to be Episcopal, and the Congregationalist ought to be Congregational; they, of all men in the world, have reason to be proud of their Congregationalism, and to stand by it. But let not Ephraim vex Judah, let not one mash against the other; love men in that respect. There is one thing that belongs to them altogether—love with a pure heart fervently, and I will trust any misleading doctrine or any ordinance or any worship, if it stands with the burning bush of love showing that the Lord God Almighty is present within.

* * *

A man that goes to heaven to escape hell is one of those men that will enter heaven "so as by fire".

* * *

Our creeds are useful in their own place. They are like stairs. If we know how to use them, they help us, step by step, to go up to the higher apartments. In their own place, which is a lowly one, where they are servants, they are useful; but when men become so much enamoured of their creeds as to make them their masters, and let them stand in the place of the truths that they are meant merely to disclose; when they are in the place of their own contents, instead of being used only as a philosophical *nexus* or outside connection—then they are usurpers.

Men ought never to worship a creed. That which it means is oftentimes worshipped without any knowledge of the creed; and that which it means is oftentimes trodden under foot by men who pretend to be defenders of the creed.

The roots of Nature are in the human mind. The life and meaning of the outward world is not in itself, but in us.

Nature implants her spirit in the human soul. Her shape is without us, her meaning is within us.

The hands of a giant upon the keys of an organ can make no more music than the hands of a common man, for the sound is in the instrument, not in the hand of the man who touches it. And the fingers of Nature, touching the faculties of the human soul, produce effects, not by the magnitude of the thing acting, but by the music within the instrument touched.

No flower blossoms, no pine stretches itself higher

toward heaven from the mountain, no cloud sails in the air, there is nothing in the field, and nothing in summer or winter, that is not of God to me.

Nature is a man's library who knows how to seek for knowledge. Nature is every man's picture gallery who knows how to hunger after and appreciate beauty. Nature is every man's portfolio, and herbarium, and garden. Nature is full of instruction to those who have a heart for knowledge.

It is as right for some persons to have the chamber of the soul unlocked by the key of Nature, as it is for others to have it unlocked by the key of the Catechism. For God is sovereign, and He works as He pleases, and He pleases to work in many ways.

We rejoice in this day, in its light, in its tranquillity, and in all the promise that it has of renewed life in all the earth. We behold the swelling bud. We hear the coming birds. We discern in sheltered places the grass greening. We believe that all around us the earth is waiting that the silent touch of God may bring resurrection to it. We are glad with each and in each other, but we desire the light of hope and cheer, of love and comfort that comes from Thee, O Thou Prince and Saviour.

It is a good thing to make it sure that we shall live hereafter; but it is also a good thing to know how to live here and now. This is simply a practice ground, and we are to live hereafter, and know that we are, by practicing those virtues which will make it possible for us to understand anything in heaven — its company, its joys, its associations.

This life is a forming, not an enjoying one. Happiness is not the end to be attained here, but manliness.

All the arrangements of our lives are parts of God's system of instruction, and they form an organic whole, of which every part is necessary to the perfectness of the whole.

The way to live is not to think about living, to do without speculating about doing.

Once, when a boy, I stood on Mount Pleasant, at Amherst, and saw a summer thunder-storm enter the valley of the Connecticut from the north. Before it all was bright; centerwise it was black as midnight, and I could see the fiery streaks of lightning striking down through it; but behind the cloud — for I could see the rear — it was bright again. In front of me was that mighty storm hurtling through the sky; and before it I saw the sunlight, and behind it I saw the sunlight; but to those that were under the center of it there was no brightness before or behind it. They saw the thunder-gust, and felt the pelting rain, and were enveloped in darkness, and heard the rush of mighty winds; but I, that stood afar off, could see that God was watering the earth, and washing the leaves, and preparing the birds for a new outcome of jubilee, and giving to men refreshment and health. So I conceive that our human life here, with its sorrows and tears, as compared with the eternity that we are going into, is no more than the breath of a summer thunder-storm; and if God sees that our experience in this world is to work out an exceeding great reward in the world to come, there is no mystery in it — to Him.

*

O, if one's life might be like the life of a skiff or yacht, or any craft or single sail in the sequestered lake, which rude winds never disturb, living would be easy; that is, it would be easy to live, if there were not so many men around; but to carry our slender bark amid currents and violent winds and constant whirls, amid rocks and bars, and amid fleets sailing in every direction — that is not easy.

⁎⁎⁎

You are worse than you think you are; you are better than you think you are. You are not doing half so much as you ought to be doing; you are doing a thousand times more than you dream of. You are working for this life too exclusively, but your work strikes through into the future life, and there is another significance given to it on the other side.

⁎⁎⁎

Life is not a grand concert which we enter to hear magnificent playing upon sweet instruments. It is more like a piano manufactory, where one hears, not music, but a confusion of noises, sawing, rattling, thumping, grating — all inharmonious sounds.

Men have reasoned on the supposition that this world is a place where we are put to be played upon. It is rather the place where those chords are made and tuned which God's own hand shall play upon, hereafter.

At midnight, undertake to examine a landscape with a candle, carrying it round to each particular thing, and try thus to get an idea of the whole scene. That is the way we are exploring in this life. But let a thunder-storm come up, and a flash of lightning opens the whole country — hill, valley, cliff, every part — to instantaneous view; and we see it instantly. That is the way we will think in the other life.

Live in the future when the present is intolerable. The future is that which lies along the path-walk of Christ, where the promises are.

Life is one grand insufficiency. Human life is like a half-finished portrait; the features marked out and hinted at, some one part, perhaps, carried further than another; but no man can determine what it is or how it shall look when it is perfected. In this life we are grinding pigments, we are collecting materials; we but dimly see, and that imperfectly. But there will come a day when I shall know even as I am known; and as God, the All-knowing, looks through and through me, and knows me altogether, I shall behold Him as He is, and all shadows and partialities will have passed away forever.

Life may not be worth living here, but may be transcendently worth living on account of the hereafter; for man is a biennial, and it takes two lives to tell him what he is. The hollyhock cannot bloom till the second season. All the first season it has no comeliness; it is coarse in leaf, undeveloped in stem, and shows no color; and the winter hushes it to rest; but the next summer brings it out, and it lifts itself up in unimagined beauty as compared with what it was in its first summer. So men are born here for a start; and they are to come to themselves only after death, and when the second summer shall find them, then they will be lifted up in unimagined glory and beauty, unless winter kills them.

This world's march is not a dumb, dull march to execution. It is not a march to a sort of clouded victory. It is a march to ethereal light by and by.

The fruitions of this world are nothing to the harvests of single kernels which will wave a hundred-fold in the other life.

Grant, we pray Thee, that we may be so intoned by the hope of the heavenly life, that we may live so near to the encouragements of it, that we shall be able to take enough out of it to uphold us in the present stress of life; that we may not only walk as seeing Him Who is invisible, but walk the realm invisible where He dwells.

A man who does not know how to live here probably will not know how to live hereafter, until after a probationary period, at any rate; and a man who knows how to live here so that his mind is kept in harmony and benevolence with all his fellowmen, seeking their interest, their good, their peace, their comfort, their ennoblement, has the very training by which a man knows how to worship God and to dwell with the pure hereafter.

***

Though every coming event may not be laid down beforehand, God will see that we come to each with all the preparation required.

***

We are not indeed to forget the future, since that would destroy the perspective of life, and take away its length, breadth and proportions. Life is an organized whole. Yesterday is the parent of to-day; to-day is the root on which to-morrow is to grow. We sleep, but the loom of life never stops, the pattern that was weaving when the sun went down is weaving still when it rises. In our plans and ideals we must live for our whole existence. The best way to prepare for the future is to hold it up while forming our plans, but to live in each day as if that were a detached whole in itself.

***

The future is a kaleidoscope; every day its glittering particles form into new combinations. We know there will be joy and sorrow, but in what forms and combinations we know not. The present has but one window out of which we can look, and that opens back into the past.

God is enthroned in the future; at every step we travel toward him. The only question is, can you be serene, faithful, just, honest, truthful and hopeful, for to-day? God will take care of to-morrow.

Grant that we may have faith to believe in the inheritance of the future. May we have confidence that our life is moving toward a land which is transcendent in all excellence, in plenitude of power, where, when we drop these mortal bodies, we shall come forth into glorious realities which but faintly appear in this life. Grant that we may feel we are living toward summer. As they that are in the far north, and wait in the darkness of winter, and rejoice to see it coming, when the sun shall again rise upon their horizon with light; so may we, wintered in time, look perpetually to death as sunrise; and may our departure hence be our emergence in the land of light.

A Christian man's life is laid in the loom of time, to a pattern which he does not see, but God does; and his heart is a shuttle. On one side of the loom is sorrow, and on the other is joy; and the shuttle struck alternately by each, flies back and forth, carrying the thread, which is white or black, as the pattern needs; and in the end, when God shall yield up the finished garment and all its changing hues shall glance out, it will then appear that the deep and dark colors were as needful to beauty as the bright and high colors.

Adversity is the mint in which God stamps upon us His image and superscription.

Not when God is lifting men up, but when He is pressing them down, is He blessing them most.

Not when he rides into the city after a victory is the general most noble, but when he is in the wilderness, and everything is dark and lowering, and by his courage and indomitable perseverance he overcomes obstacles. It is when a man rises above his circumstances and moods that true manhood shows itself in him. It is then he is grandest and nearest to God.

When God brings men into this world in a crude state, as sand and kelp are brought into the manufactory; or when, like crude iron, they are subjected to the transforming influences of this trip-hammer life, by which they are thumped, and jammed, and cut, and haggled, and pricked, and bruized, he does it that moral results may be evolved on a large scale.

You shall find that they who are free from hardships, from troubles, from the necessity of endeavor, and who never struggled with adversity of any kind, cannot be relied upon for sills and posts. They may do for veneering the inside, when you want something pretty, but they are good for nothing else.

There are some steamers that are built so that they do not rise over the wave; they jam their nose right into it, as if they would plough the whole ocean. The consequence is, that their decks are always wet, and everybody is always sick. There are other steamers that lift themselves to everything that comes, and ride over the waves, and are as sweet as a cradle.

It is a great thing to teach men how to ride over trouble; and it is a very painful thing to see men dashing their noses into the waves, and insisting upon going through them, when they could a great deal easier go over them.

No man can become a man that has not been ground more or less. It is grinding that destroys the blunt edges, and makes men sharp.

* * *

When the sculptor stands before a block of marble, I can imagine that the unlucent and unintelligent stone might say, "I was promised to be made a godlike figure and put into a public niche to be admired; yet here, day by day, there is a rude, brutal fellow with his sharp chisel and heavy mallet, knocking off pieces from me, and when he has got down so that even my form appears, still he is knocking my face and cutting me here and there." That is the way that works of art are made. It is by things that they lose that the features come out and their proportions are made to appear. God is a great artist. And if there are any of you that are to be statues in the niches of heaven, God, probably, is chiselling you, and you ought, at least, by this time, to understand something about God's dealings with you; that by your care, by your burdens, by your sorrows, and by your losses, He is teaching you that this world is not your home, and that the other life is; that you are not fit for it yet, and He is, as it were, like a sculptor, unburdening you of the superfluous stone that is in you, and letting out the lineaments and beauty of your hidden life.

A man that is bankrupt when his property goes has not been a man. To be a true man, surrounded with true riches, one should be able to say, "I am richer inside than I am outside." There is many and many a man who, like an athlete, does not go into the arena for high conflict until he has stripped himself of all encumbering clothes, and stands in his nakedness, that every muscle may have free play in his conflict with some adversary. There are men that never seem so noble and strong as when God has stripped them of all their possessions, and left nothing but them; and the grandest thing there is this side of the throne of God is a man.

The man who plans for himself in life that there shall not be any hills in his road, that he is going to travel on a level plain, that there is not going to be any gravel in his shoes, that there are not to be any stones in his way, and that he is not going to have any color taken out of his serene face — that man has an antagonist that he does not suspect; it is God — Who has decreed that he shall bear burdens, and that he shall work out his own salvation, and develop his own manhood.

Ah! the loss of things in this world is oftentimes great gain. Have you noticed that frequently in the abundance of the leaves of summer, both the landscape and the mansion are hidden? Though it is a sad time, and we do not like to see the leaves turn sere; though we dread the coming of the frosts, yet behold, when, in the morning after the frost, every tree is bare, and not a leaf is left; as we look, there appears a house that we have not seen all summer. The leaves hid it; the landscape — the mountains and the distant river — which has so long been obscured, is revealed to us. What a wonderful vision is opened when the leaves fall!

Many and many a man, whose prosperity has been like thick foliage before his eyes, could not see his Father's house, had no view of the heavenly Jerusalem, nor of the beautiful landscape beyond; but when adversity came and stripped him bare, and people said, "He is gone! he is gone!" he was richer than he ever had been before.

We pray to God to make us strong, meaning, drop down some invisible strength through the air into our souls. God answers our prayer by laying upon us a burden, and says, "Stand up". But we cannot stand up under it without growing strong.

When the Ohio river is at its lowest ebb there are places which a boy could ford, going across with perfect ease and safety; but in the spring, when the snow melts on the Alleghanies, and the water comes pouring down, the channel between the banks is filled so that neither man nor beast can cross it. And when the mightier storms come on, the Ohio swells and rises still higher, and overflows the banks, and covers the lowlands, and men drive their cattle up on higher ground, and take refuge there themselves. And when the greater freshets come, the inhabitants go on climbing higher and higher until they reach points where the flood cannot reach them.

So, when the overflowing storms of reverse and disappointment overcome you, do not sit still and be drowned; and do not float like water-logged sticks, too long cut, soaked and rotten, and good for nothing; but rise so high that no flood and no envenomed shaft can reach you; so high that heaven shall be your home, that you shall be in the presence of God, and that that spiritual manhood shall be yours which can see no corruption.

* * *

O ye that mourn because you are cut off from the work of life! What is the work of life? Is it building St. Peter's? It may be that. It may also be ploughing the field.

Either by ploughing the field or building the temple we may be ministering to our higher manhood, and to the welfare of others.

He that builds a higher manhood is doing the work of God; whether he constructs an edifice or tills the soil.

If you want the sweetest of flowers — the trailing arbutus — you will not find it on the tops of churches; you will not find it on walls of brick; you will not find it in cultivated places where the resources of the farmer's skill and ingenuity have been expended; you will not find it on the lofty hills. It humbly creeps along the edges of the forest where the soil is dry, and not rich. Before the snow is completely gone you may find it nestling down under the leaves, ready to burst forth in the spring; and when it has come forth, it has a beauty with which nothing else can vie. Blessed be the winter, blessed be the snow, and blessed be the covering leaves, dry, withered, under which lie such exquisite blossoms.

God's flower-bed is oftentimes your sick-bed; for patience, a sweet resignation, faith that looks beyond the visible, and that development of a true manhood which sickness often brings out in its royalty and fulness—these things are better than any outward achievement.

Woe to the man who has everything brought to him; and blessed are they who are born under adverse circumstances, and have no chance in life; and who, instead of whining because they have no chance, develop an inward manhood that gives them a chance — for there is that in man which dominates over chance, time and nature. A man can make himself sovereign if he has but the purpose.

Old trees stand on mountain sides, and that the wind plays harp with through winter and summer, grow strong, so that the tornado cannot wrest them from their places. Oaks that are anchored among the rocks, the earthquake itself cannot dislodge. They grow massive through the centuries. But take the palm-tree that never has been outside of the conservatory. It is brought up with no more agitation than a bee makes when flying in its branches. And how much can it bear? If the gardener but leaves the door open for a single night, and the frost comes to it, it is gone. It has no stamina. It is softened by the things that made it grow so fat.

While outward blessings are an advantage, the loss of all things may be a higher one. There are thousands of men destroyed because they have so much.

All our noblest inspirations are but as tapers, and the great sun of the other life shall throw them into darkness. Whatever is bright and transcendent in nobleness here, is dim in the light of the reality there.

Among the farces men act is the trying to ascertain whether they are Christians or not, by inquiring whether they are willing to die. It is a duty to feel like living while you live; when God wants you to die, the chariot will be waiting.

The valley of the shadow of Death is not dreadful

to those who pass through it, but to those who follow after, but may not pass through.

Death is a strainer; and there are multitudes of things that men value here which are rubbish at the mouth of the grave. They are not permitted to go through.

The grave is God's bankrupt court, which clears a man of his property and his debts at the same time.

O, may the sun pierce through the shade of trees, dear to many birds, to fall in checkered light upon my grave! I ask no stone or word of inscription. May flowers be the only memorial of my grave, renewed every spring, and maintained through the summer.

To every truly Christian experience the grave is as a telescope, and as a magnifying glass, through which the world beyond and the triumph over this world are being celebrated.

At the grave we shall leave all that this world has

given us, we carry out only what the soul has in itself, of honor, purity, nobleness; if we have allowed ourselves to be cheated there, we go out paupers, eternally bankrupt.

***

Death is the swelling of the seed that has lived here, that is dried up and is waiting for its planting. Death is the bursting of the bud in April that all winter long has lain tight bound within itself, waiting for its life of efflorescence. Death is entering on summer from the frigid zone.

***

The door of death is the door of hope; the grave is that lens through which we see immortality.

***

It is a man dying with his harness on that angels love to take.

***

The perfection that God thinks of is not simply fulfilling a few laws and restraining a few appetites. It is growth, it is largeness of thought, largeness of heart, largeness of disposition; and no man yet living upon earth, save Him who descended from above and called Himself the equal of the eternal God, has ever reached anything like perfection. A man may have overcome the ordinary accidents and temptations of life, but growth and blossom await us. Buds may appear here, and some few flowers, but not until we are transplanted and see God as He is, and breathe the pure atmosphere of the eternal summer, and are surrounded by all the saints in glory, shall any one of us be able to say, "I am perfect. I see Him as He is, and I am like Him."

No eloquence is like that of a fact of soul-experience. What God is doing within us, is the most dramatic thing that is going on in all the world. There are dramas of passion, there are dramas of history; but the silent dramas of the summer of the soul are more wonderful than any others that are taking place on earth; and these are the ones that mostly slumber, and are not brought out in speech.

The best deeds in every department of life of those that have gone before, are embalmed and transmitted as legacies unspeakably precious. Pearls and diamonds, and precious stones of every name, are not to be compared with those richer jewels of the soul, which here and there, though too rarely, have flashed out their light in days gone by.

*
* *

Great souls know each other. Years are the servitors of slower natures, and nurse them into mutual confidences. There are certain touches that fine natures know instantly, conclusive of all the rest—the free-masonry of the sons of God!

The rapture of true love in souls on earth at first finding themselves each other's, the glory and pride of finding one's self loved, the conscious swelling in us of another life mightier than we knew before being loved—this is the only experience that will at all shadow forth the communion of man's soul with God. It is the war of Spirit with Spirit.

He that reads by the outward eye does not see half that is written in this world. The spirit reads one thing, and the flesh another.

The soul, when it gathers its strength and feels its own majesty, rises above the trifling accidents of life and rides triumphantly over them as an ark over a flood.

The soul sits in the human body as great commercial cities sit upon the sides of the sea; and as every climate and every land on the earth send forth their various productions to them, and as all things report themselves in these great commercial citadels, so the soul, an open harbor, receives from all the universe its stores and its tributes.

There is in domestic sorrow a delicacy, or ought to be, which should shrink from an ostentatiousness such as mourning apparel cannot fail to have.

No one has a right so to express his sorrows as to intrude them upon every eye wherever he goes.

Autumnal days are the most beautiful days of the year, and they ought to be the most beautiful days in a man's life. In October things do not grow any more, they ripen, they fulfill the destiny of the summer, and the thought of autumn is that it is going down, going forth. When all things in Nature know and feel that death is coming near, do they sheet themselves in black, as pagan Christians do? Do they turn everything to hideous mourning, as pagan Christians do? They cry, "Bring forth our royal garments"; and the oak puts on the habiliments of beauty, and all the herbs of the field turn to scarlet and yellow and every color that is most precious; and the whole month of autumn goes tramping toward death, glowing and glorious. It is only men that make death hateful and gloomy and black—servants of midnight the whole of them.

⁎⁎⁎

No man ever yet learnt by having somebody else learn for him. A man learns arithmetic by blunder in and blunder out, but at last he gets it. A man learns to write through scrawling; a man learns to swim by going into the water, and a man learns to vote by voting. We are not attempting to make a government; we are attempting to teach sixty millions of men how to conduct a government by self-control, by knowledge, by intelligence, by fair opportunity to practice. It is better that we should have sixty millions of men learning through their own mistakes how to govern themselves, than it is to have an arbitrary government with the whole of the rest of the people ignorant.

⁎⁎⁎

Voting is an art. It is like rifle-shooting—a man misses a good many times before he learns to hit.

⁎⁎⁎

What are called woman's rights are simply the rights of human beings, and before a woman can do right and well in the direction of humanity and virtue she has a right to vote. I hold that a woman has the right to vote; but if you withhold from her on any considerations of supposed propriety voting for the remote questions of civility, there is one sphere where a woman is not allowed to vote, and where she ought to have a vote. She brings forth children in pain, she spends and squanders her life on them, bringing them up from infancy and helplessness to manhood and strength; and if there is one creature on the earth that has a right to vote what sort of school there should be in a district, what teacher should be there, for how many months it should be kept open, what should be taught in it — if there is one person who has a right to speak of the gambling dens and drinking hells that are round about her family, it is the mother of the children, and in all police relations and educational matters, and everything that touches the virtue and morality of society, our civilization will not be perfected until it should be, as it is in religion, that man and woman stand before God equal and alike.

The ballot — the silent fall of those flakes of paper, which come as snow comes, soundless, but which gather, as snow gathers on the tops of the mountains, to roll with the thunder of the avalanche, and crush all beneath it.

The corruption of the ballot is a blow at the very heart of public liberty. The result is liable to be, not the unbiased expression of the popular will, but the fulfillment of the wishes of tricksters and unprincipled politicians.

The way to teach a man to vote is to let him vote; the way to teach a man archery is to let him shoot; to look at a match will never teach him to shoot.

There are a great many generous people that are not liberal, and there are a great many liberal people that are not generous. A man is liberal when, taking a large view, he follows his higher judgment in regard to objects of relief or of donation. He does not need to see; he has a large circumspection of causes and influences, and so he is liberal. But a man that is generous, generally follows his senses. He wants to hear the cry, to see the poverty, to feel the loss. Anything that he can hear, and see, and feel, and observe, he has the impulse of kindness toward, and that is being generous. A great many men are very hard and cold; they are liberal, but they have no generosity, and they have no credit for being even liberal. Generosity is the senses working with kindness, while liberality is faith working with kindness, which is much larger.

Some have supposed that a meek man was one who, when he was hit, just did not hit back. I despise such meekness as that. To be lean and rat-like, running round in the holes of life, is not to be meek.

Meekness is that great luminousness which the complete ascendancy of all the higher and nobler instincts of man gives to the whole expression of his life — to his eye, to his face, to his words, to his deeds. It is the richness of the Divine elements in a man that makes him illustrious and beautiful.

Men are seldom true to themselves or entirely natural in their prayers.

A prayer is not a thread on which men are to see how many texts they can string.

Many prayers are rolling full of O's, and the voice runs through half a semi-circular scale of gracious intonation with every other sentence. It is — O, do this, and O, do that, O, send, O, give, O, bless, O, help, O, search, O, look, O, smile, O, come, O, forgive, O, spare, O, hear, O, let, O, snatch, O, watch — O! O! O! through the whole petition with every variety of inflection.

We pray that Thou wilt be with those who have troubles of heart; who are necessitous; whose better nature trembles and is afraid; who every day look up with anxious thoughts. O, Lord! Thou that didst bear the cross, dost Thou give them an empty cross? Has any soul ever come and taken Thy cross, that Thou wert not with it and beneath it, to bear it? How many have taken that cross as of dry and seasoned wood, and found it springing forth and clasping them with a thousand tendrils and branches, every branch full of fruit, till they were embowered and embosomed in that which seemed to them a task, or labor! Draw near to all those who are in any trouble of mind, and so magnify Thyself unto them that their trouble shall not be able to abide. When quiet days come, then comes the dust that settles on the fairest things; but when rousing winds come, then comes cleansing, and the dirt is blown away. Send, we beseech Thee, that wind from heaven which shall take away the dust of care and the grime of trouble from us, and give us clear skies at last between our souls and Thine.

I pray on the principle that the wine knocks the cork out of a bottle. There is an inward fermentation, and there must be a vent somewhere. It is the soul that prays first; the tongue may afterwards.

Prayer is never to be a substitute for exertion. It is never to take the place of education. Prayer is asking God to use the enginery of Nature, the enginery of society, and above all, the enginery of our souls in our behalf. Men say, "God is not going to stop the universe to answer prayer". No; but he is going to work the universe in order to answer prayer. I cannot stand in my wheat field and say, "O, wheat, come up", and have an immediate answer to my prayer; but if I want wheat, I know how I can get it. There are certain laws of Nature, I know, and I know that the operation of these laws is inevitable and sure, and I can call up blessings by using them upon myself, upon my family and upon my neighbors; for to-day, for the year to come and for a whole generation.

Any trouble that a man would go to his earthly father about, he may go to God about. People say: "Do you believe that, contrary to all the great laws of Nature, and political economy, God will provide a sum of money for a man in answer to his prayer? Do you believe that God controvenes natural laws to assist a man in paying his debts?" I do not. But when a man has used his means to the uttermost, and trusts in God, then God uses his means to control natural laws for that man's benefit. God helps men not by stopping natural laws, but by using them better for us than we can use them for ourselves. And when a man is in trouble, and goes to God and says, "I have done all I can, I do not know what to do more, I am willing to suffer or to be relieved — 'Thy will be done'." I believe that then God hears and answers prayer, even though of a secular nature.

* * *

Prayer is not simply a desire that we may have that which in the present hour we may need. It is a sense of our alliance with our heavenly Father. It is an endeavor to be in such converse with Him as a child is during the hour of its joy, or its sorrow, or of its burden, in the presence of its earthly parent. It is lifting up the soul out of matter, and out of its poor surroundings, into the presence and sympathy of the Spirit of God, the great Love and Lover.

* * *

Prayer is not the voice of a beggar. It is not simply the expression of want. It is the expression in our best hours, and in our best moods, of the best thoughts, the best sentiments, the best emotions, the best aspirations, the best of everything. If the soul be a mighty estate; if it hath everything of flower and fruit in it, we bring something of everything and the best, and offer it to God.

* * *

Prayer chiefly, is the soul's communion with God. It is chiefly translation. It is chiefly transfiguration. It was worth more to Peter and James and John, to stand for an hour and see the spirits dawn through the heaven, and talk with Christ, Whose face shone as the sun, and Whose raiment was white as light, than if the three tabernacles which they craved had been built of diamonds and rubies on the mountain-top. It is what we get by the soul that makes us rich.

As birds that are low down in dusky forests, and are chased by owls, escape in the broad sunlight, so our souls, when they are in low, dark places, flying away from these up toward God, find release, and sing for joy.

Prayer is not so much an office, as it is the soul's whole attitude toward God, so that everything which one does, he does in conscious communion with God.

I think the answer to prayer is that which gives inspiration to the souls of men; and he who walks in the presence of God, and lives under the inspiration of His down-brooding touch, has in himself the great causes which will work out the answers of prayer — and that in the higher spheres, as well as in the lower.

You can draw a stop of an organ, and it will give the sound which belongs to that stop; but you cannot do the same thing with the soul. If you would enjoy the richest fruits of prayer, you must abound in prayer; you must live in the conscious presence of God; you must be in constant and intimate communion with Him. Then there can be no doubt, no skepticism in your mind as to the efficacy of prayer.

Where men begin their prayers by piling up old, long, familiar, worn, empty titles; where they commence their prayers by saying, "O, Thou omnipotent, omniscient, omnipresent, all-seeing, ever-living, blessed Potentate, Lord God Jehovah!" I should think they would take breath. "Why," it is asked, "are not such titles as these right?" Yes; but what should be the state of a man's mind when he can fill up such big words as these with the reality of their meaning? That there are extreme moods, that there are great and critical times, when God has, by the breaths of heaven and the currents of earth, moved men in the higher elements; that there are periods when these words are as majestic as God Himself in the souls of men, there is no doubt; but think of a man in his family, hurried for his breakfast or to get away to his business, praying in such a strain! He has a note coming due, and it is going to be paid to-day; and he feels buoyant, and goes down on his knees like a cricket on the hearth, and piles up these majestically moving phrases about God. Then he goes on to say, with hasty formality, that he is a sinner. Yes, he is proud to say that he is a sinner. He goes with the multitude in this respect. Then he asks that he may be forgiven, and that his heart may be changed. And then he asks for his daily bread. He has it; and he can always ask for it when he has it. After running on thus briefly in the old stereotyped way, he winds up with, "For thine is the kingdom, and the power and the glory, forever and forever, Amen". Then he jumps up, and goes over to the city, and attends to his business affairs. At night he comes back, and if he is not disturbed by sleepiness, by company or something else, he has evening prayers; but he never thinks of approaching his Father in heaven in any other than this hard, formal, matter-of-fact way. And he is called a "praying man!" I should sooner call myself an ornithologist because I ate a chicken once in a while for my dinner. In outside affairs, does occasionally having something to do with them constitute an acquaintance with them? Does any man really pray who does not know the inner man that belongs to his nature? Does any man pray in reality who has not a consciousness of God present with him? He that goes to God "must believe that He is, and that He is a rewarder of them that diligently seek Him". How large is the interpretation of that saying! He that goes to God, goes to One whom the heavens cannot contain, nor the earth, which is His footstool. How lordly is the soul that mounts up into some sort of conception of the amplitude, the grandeur, the glory and the desirableness of the Father in heaven!

Prayer works not on narrow lines. It consists not

simply of asking for something. It works through a celestial magnetizing of the whole soul. It lifts a man above the infirmities of the flesh. It brings him into the region of supernal power. It gives him the inspiration of God Himself.

*

God answers prayer just as in Nature he answers the wishes of the husbandman. He makes the clouds to rain, and the sun to shine; and forth from the earth come ten thousand voices of birds and insects, singing and chirping, making the air vocal, and filling our hearts full of song.

And all things grow and flourish under the influence of the great vivifying Force of Nature. So when we walk with God, and live with Him, our prayers are answered, whatever we may ask for, because to love, all things are lawful. We pray for whatever we want, because we love God, because we are near to Him, because we adore Him, and because we are enraptured with the thought of His glory; and he sends answers to our prayers through ourselves, and outside of ourselves, in ten thousand ways. It is not half so much importance that we should know how the thing comes, as that we should know that the thing does come—peace, rest, purity, hope, aspiration, courage in darkness, insight into the life to come; the prolongation of our manhood into the eternal sphere, that we may feel the crown before ever it is put upon our head; that we may hear songs before ever they are uttered by us, sung by those who await us in heaven.

That which is immortal in us has not time to ripen in the short summer of this world.

Generosity is kindness drawn out by the sight of need. It is the ministration of our senses in the work of kindness. Liberality provides for that need which is not seen, which our superior reason foresees or imagines. One acts as an emotion, the other as a judgment. The one is of the heart, the other is of the intellect as well as of the heart. One moves in a circuit of material things, the other is aeriform. The conjunction of the two furnishes the noblest form of benevolence — that which works both by sight and by faith.

Generosity is a glorious thing, but it is not everything; it is inferior to liberality, and certainly it is inferior to both liberality and generosity. Liberality for the husband, generosity for the wife; that is, they ought to be married to each other, and then they form a perfect unity.

Generosity works by sight; liberality works by faith.

Never deliberate on your word, but let it go as the arrow goes to the target—let it strike and stand.

Words are but the bannerets of a great army; thoughts are the main body of the future. Words show here and there a little gleam in the air, but the great multitude of thoughts march unseen below.

* * *

How much of thought there is in cultivated men! How much of thought that goes for thin language! But how much more thought that never rides in the chariot of language! How much men think day by day that is only thinking!

In my orchards to-day, there are, I think, on single cherry-trees thousands of blossoms; and probably all but about a hundred or two of those will drop without a cherry having formed under them. Men are like such trees. They breed thoughts by the millions, that result in action only in the scores and the hundreds. How much of thought and feeling is there, and what an incessant work is going on within the sensorium of the body, among men! How many angers, how many griefs, how many hopes, how many wishes, how many purposes; what ranges of speculation, what building of plans, some on the ground, and some in the air!

What wonderful goods are being woven — more wonderful than by the Jacquard loom — in the manufactory of the head; and yet how little ever comes forth into the merchant's salesroom, how little is ever visible! We think, I suppose, a hundred times more than we ever put into action, or put into language, into visible exponential form.

* *
*

Folk's good and bad is like a board-teeter — if one end goes up, t'other is sure to go down.

* *
*

No person is born great. If a man becomes great, it is by that struggle in life by which he develops himself.

* *
*

Greatness consists not in what one has, but in what use one makes of his possessions — not in capacity, but in a right exercise of that capacity.

* *
*

Doubt and faith are born twins, and you have no right to separate them. They ought to recognize each other. Doubt of things past is simply clearing the way to a brighter and a nobler future; and since with the spirit of knowledge, old things are passing away, let us thank God, and only ask that the doubters may become the new men of a generation of faith.

Right in front of my house I have a beech-tree. All winter long, because its leaves were so beautiful during the summer, it holds on to them. In January they are there; in February they are there; in March they are there. In May the tree begins to grow and one after the other the leaves begin to drop. There is nothing that will undo the old dead leaf that has no juice in it, so quickly as growth in the tree. When men are growing, the old leaves begin to drop off. It is not a sign of decadence; it is a sign that summer is coming, that the tree is growing larger, and the gloss on the old leaves is a mere prophecy of the coming of new ones, fresher ones, brighter ones.

The skepticism of honest men unfolds the truth, and becomes the conviction of the after-time. The unbelief of to-day is the faith of to-morrow.

Paul was a moral genius. There are moral geniuses just as much as there are musical or artistic. Prayer is as much an original gift of genius with many men as poetry is with others. Spiritual insight is a gift; that is, some men have genius in that direction. Some men have genius in dealing with matter, and some have genius in the direction of mind or formative power. Paul was a genius in every direction, and one of the most wonderful moral natures which ever came upon earth.

***

Science is a cane, religion is the man that walks with it, and helps himself along the rough road of life.

***

The future is not in danger from the revelations of science. Science is Truth. Truth loves truth. Changes must come, and old things must pass away, but no tree sheds its leaf until it has rolled up a bud at its axil, for the next summer.

***

Science is but the deciphering of God's thought as revealed in the structure of this world; it is a mere translation of God's primitive revelation. If to reject God's revelation of the Book is infidelity, what is it to reject God's revelation of Himself in the structure of the whole globe? There is as much infidelity in regard to the great history that science unfolds to-day, as there is in regard to the record of the Book — and more! The primitive prefatory revelation of the structural thought of God in preparing a dwelling for the human race — is that nothing? Man had a cradle represented to antiquity as the poetical Eden ; but the globe itself had a different Eden — one of fire, convulsions, clouds and storms, of grinding ice and biting chemistry preparing the soil.

* * *

I believe that in our day God is revealing Himself by the hands of the natural philosophers. I am not alarmed at what may be called the personal infidelity of these men. They are all workers together, though they do not know it.

Go with me to a silk factory, and take down one of the most exquisite pieces of silk and unroll it. Oh, what a beautiful pattern! What fineness of texture! What exquisite colors! What magnificent figures! Why, it is charming!

Now let us see how it is made. We will go back step by step till we come to the loom where it was woven. We see this machine, that does not know what it is doing, throwing its shuttles by some operation which it cannot understand. Let us go further back. We see men in one of the rooms punching holes here and there in a pasteboard card, according to some plan which has been devised; and these holes mean figures. When the fabric is put on the loom in the proper way, in certain places given colors and given threads come out, according to these holes. The idea that they have any relation to the making of that silk, or helping to make it, seems perfectly absurd. But go further back, and you will find men spinning silk, and working on little bits of thread; and if you are told that they are making such a fabric as that, you say, "They are not; they are spinning single threads". What they are doing has not the slightest relation, apparently, to the fabric. Go back further yet, and you will find men up to their elbows in nasty-looking dye-stuff, in a badly smelling room, and all smouched themselves. I say, "You recollect those exquisite colors which you saw; those men are making them". On going further back we find boys and girls, six, eight or ten of them, winding up little bits of films from yellow cocoons. These boys are talking and laughing with each other, and I say, "They are working for that silk fabric". "Do not tell me any such stuff as that!"

I take you one step further back. We go into the cocoonery where there is craunching that sounds like rain falling on a roof, and I show you millions of little ugly-looking worms, and say, "These are the folks, after all, that are making the silk". "What! these worms?" "Yes, these worms."

Now, then, take a Christian, according to the ordinary acceptation of that term. A Christian in this world is — well, a minister, or a deacon, that knows all theology, and keeps Sunday, and observes all the proprieties of the sanctuary, and lives an admirable, blameless life, and holds the faith of the Church exactly right. Men look on such a man, and say, "There, that is what I call a regular churchman, and a good Christian man". I present to them Herbert Spencer; and they say, "What! that outrageous skeptic, Herbert Spencer? He, mentioned in the same day with that excellent Christian man — that admirable churchman?" I present to them John Stuart Mill. "Why!" they say, "he did not believe in a God, even." So these worms did not know they were making silk. They did not believe in silk. If you had told them about silk they could not have understood you.

What fools you are! What a fool I am! What fools all men are! How preposterously we reason about things! Do you suppose everything in the world is going to run according to your pendulum? Is there not a common scheme which regulates the affairs of this globe? And are not all men working in obedience to that scheme, and working in their own way, God being the great Architect? Is not everybody working, whether he knows it or not, toward the final consummation of things.

If religion is the truth of God in its essence and absolute reality, it never can be rubbed out; and I am not afraid. Those who work most to rub it out are often those who do most to diffuse it, and cleanse it, and bring it into power.

*
* *

One may imagine a musical instrument left in some old castle deserted during political revolutions, standing warped and cracked with heat and dampness—unstrung, untuned and voiceless. But at length the owner returns, and the tuner is summoned to put the instrument in order. He lifts the cover and the dust rolls back in clouds. "Ah!" he says, "it is a noble instrument, by the grandest of makers."

He strikes a chord — a hideous discord, rather — which drives all hearers from the place. And now, as he begins to screw and turn, to bring up each key to its proper pitch, what wailings and screechings fill the room. People would say, "That a musical instrument?" But the tuner says, "Wait, all will be right in time!" And when the long work is completed and he sits down to draw forth from those strings some melody, or one of Beethoven's majestic harmonies, children and servants flock to listen in amazement and wonder. Thus it is with us in this world. O, be patient while God is tuning you. Now the wailing and the discord, by and by the full and perfect harmony.

Troubles are like mosquitoes. Some nervous people spend far more effort to drive off little insect trials than would be needed to bear them. Why do they not pray, "Lord, let Thy grace be sufficient for me"? That is a piece of armor that would cover them from head to foot. It is a great deal better to bear trouble than to get rid of trouble.

There are many men that will not get away from trouble when they can. If there is trouble in one room, they will not so much as go into another room to avoid it. A wise man, when he finds himself in a room where there is trouble, goes out of it as soon as possible. Now God has put at least thirty rooms in a man's mind, and if there is trouble in one, he can go up to the next one, and if the trouble comes into that, he can go up to the next, and if necessary, he can keep going up-stairs till he gets upon the roof; and the higher he goes, the more tired will troubles get of flying up after him.

Troubles are like mists that fill a river valley in an Autumn morning, hanging chilly and damp upon the hillsides until the sun gets high in the heavens, then swaying, wreathing, opening, they melt away at length into the clear air. As the sun is to the mists so is the soul of man to his troubles, when touched and inspired of God. When from the heights of faith and hope we look steadily down into our sorrows, they quickly take to themselves wings and fly away.

Manhood is the most precious fruit of trouble. There is but one tree in this world that bears true, full manhood. You cannot go and take any tree and plant it at hazards, and get spitzenbergs from it. If you want spitzenbergs, you must plant a tree that will bear spitzenbergs; and if you want russets, you must plant a tree that bears russets. There is one tree, and only one, that bears true manhood; and if you want true manhood, you must have that tree. And that tree is trouble.

Nothing is half so medicinal for our troubles as benevolent sympathy and occupation in the troubles of others. This is the true moral recreation.

Sorrows are gardeners; they plant flowers along waste places, and teach vines to cover barren heaps. The common duties of life, unblessed, are but as fences of stone, or timber; but blessed with sorrow, each stake carries its twining morning-glory, and mosses picture the stones, and glowing ampelopsis tufts the walls with its autumnal red.

Forbearance, courage, toughness, endurance, the ability to meet trouble and not be vanquished by it, but tranquilly rejoice in it, are elements of manhood.

Among the branches, now clearly seen, is a nest, hidden all summer by green leaves, all the autumn by golden ones — a nest, an empty nest! When it was a home, and gay birds inhabited it, green leaves hid from dangerous eyes the treasure. When its work was done, golden leaves hid its emptiness. The tree is bare, the nest is empty, November days are chill;

but the birds hatched therein have flown over hill and over field, and are singing far away upon the southern trees. They will come back! Next summer the leaves will hide again the nest, and the merry brood will come again from it. Yet empty nests there are, to which will come again no wing, no song. Too well they flew, and were carried clear over into the eternal summer. "I shall go to him, but he will not return unto me." Thus spoke the kingly singer of Israel, and ten thousand hearts repeat the solemn liturgy.

I do not know what my children will be to me when I am in heaven; but this one thing I know, that the heavenly experience will not be behind the earthly one. I shall find them; they will find me; and they will be more to me there than they ever were here. I do not know how, but there was a wonderful hold upon my soul of the little children that could do nothing but love, and that but faintly. The wound — how deep it was! how long in healing! and how, while it was yet unhealed, I thought, "I cannot spare them. They will grow up; they will be full grown; but I want my children, I want my children."

You do not know what the wondrous elasticity and versatility of disembodied existence is. You do not know but your children will come to you and be more children than ever they were, except in stature and capacity. All that has made them sweet and lovely to you may be more than ever, along with an aureola, a coronal light of love and beauty.

* * *

Do you ever notice the dandelion when it first comes up in the spring, and is nothing but a mat of little, flat and homely leaves, lying snugly on the ground? A few days of summer sun will bring out the plaited bud, nippled in the soil. In a few days more, it will lift itself higher, and open its golden circle. It is now born; and so are our children born to us. Wait yet a few days, and that blossom is shut up. Its beauty is gone. Wait a few days again, and out it comes once more. But now it is an airy globe. White as pearl and exquisite in form, as no compass could score it. An ethereal globe it is. The wind could blow it away. And such are our children. They have gone from us, beautiful to the last. Through all ages they shall live, and bud and blossom. They have been wafted away to the celestial sphere, where they are singing, and shall sing forever and forever. Sons of God are your children, and they are with God.

* * *

Not any bower of roses is so festooned in June. Not where the jessamine and honeysuckle twine, and lovers sit, is there so fair a sight, so sweet a prospect, as where a soul, in its early years, is flying away out of life, and out of time, through the gate of death — the rosy gate of death, the royal gate of death, the golden gate of death, the pearly gate of death.

* * *

I think God makes men, in some respects, as He makes tulips. In the autumn of the year the next year's blossom is stored up, all ready to come forth, and there is food enough in it to get it out of the ground. Children are bulbs. There is parent enough in them to last till they can organize character for themselves.

* * *

How fair is the world which Thou hast made, O Lord, our God! How wonderful art Thou in Thy glory, and in all Thy thoughts of beauty, and in all the excellence which the earth doth show forth. And yet, where hast Thou made anything so beautiful or so full of sweetness as little children are? They are of Thee and they bear something of Thy nature, and shall go back to Thee to report what history hath befallen them on earth. They are Thine, and they are lent to us. And what joy do they bring! Though they come crying, how they do come to bear smiles and laughter, and full-handed joy! How light is the house with them, and how dark it is without them! How full of strength dost Thou make their little weakness to those who are called to take care of them! How in nourishing them do we nourish ourselves! How in teaching them do we ourselves learn! How we are taught what God is by that which He makes us to be by those little ones that are so dear to us.

Children don't come up and blossom first like hyacinths and that great red amaryllis. They are like laylocks and honeysuckle, that grow a year or two before they get a place for blossoms to stand on.

We are apt to put too many blades in our knives nowadays. I would rather give a boy a handle and let him put in his own blade. There is nothing like working out a thing yourself. Lead is as good as steel when the knife is in your pocket. Put it to hard work and see which keeps its edge — that tells the difference between good temper and none at all.

No poet, no philosopher, can tell what is the richness and fruitfulness and wonder of the imagination that hovers over a Christian woman's cradle. To her, the star of the East comes again to stand over where the young child lies. To her, the wise men of the earth might well come, bearing offerings and incense. To her, again are renewed all the scenes of the sacred stable where the Child lay. The cradle is her temple, the baby is her Divinity. And whatever reason can, and whatever fancy can, when both of them are stimulated by profoundest love, whatever there is near or far, present or to come, that love is woman's. "Mary kept these things in her heart and pondered them." The pondering of a mother! If it could be written, if there were any angelic reporter band to take the best thoughts and the sweetest fancies, and if the life of a mother's heart could be written in those early brooding days, it would shine fit to be read in the libraries of the heavenly world itself. Human nature never comes so near to the Divine, as when a royal woman pours out the full flood of her thought and fancy and love to the little unheeding, and to her, as yet, useless child. Where else is she so beautiful as when she sits in the center of this mystic circle, as when she sings to her babe, or gazes silently as it feeds upon her bosom? The stars have nothing so bright, and the heavens scarcely anything more pure and more holy than the heavenly love-service of a mother to her little helpless and unfashioned child.

Some people seem to think that a child is like a farm, and cannot be pulverized too much; and so they plough it, and harrow it, and cross it, and turn it up and down as it does not like to be turned.

Wedded love has its burdens and exceptions. The cradle none. We love and are loved again; we pass through the dream of early love when all is paradisiacal; and at last, according to the old myth, we fall, and discover that our angel was human. It was a pure and perfect diamond! Alas! some day there are flaws found in it. Henceforth we bear and forbear; we suffer that we may love. Not so the cradle. There is no dross in that gold; there is no commerce there; there is no giving and taking. The heart, like a smitten rock, flows with a pure and undiminished stream, even in the deserts of poverty. There is no love that is so spontaneous that hath in it so little of the influence and motive which actuates every other part of life, as the simple, indispensable, irresistible love which parents have for new-born children, and at every step onward until they begin to be men and women.

You can't tell by the way a bean comes up what sort of leaves it's goin' to have afterwards. Some children are like poke-weed. When it first comes up it's just as good to bile as 'sparagus. But in a few weeks it's so strong it would drive ye out of the house, if you was to put it in the pot.

***

If every child might live the life pre-destined in a mother's heart, all the way from the cradle to the coffin, they would walk upon a beam of light, and shine in glory. Alas! some are born like the dandelion — glowing bright, soon changing to a fairy globe, and by the first wind dashed out and gone! Paint the man as the mother's thoughts do; then paint him as he really lived! Hang the two portraits side by side, and write, "What he was to be!" and then, "What he was!" Life has no sadder contrast.

As men whose lamp has gone out are in the darkness of familiar rooms, and grope and know not how to find their way, so dost Thou often by sorrow bewilder Thy people; and yet, speak unto them, O God! that they may know that Thou art present, and that they may rejoice in the midst of great pain and suffering.

We are not to covet or seek pain; but we are not to dodge it when it comes. We should feel that God puts confidence in us when He lays a heavy burden upon us. A general sends no coward to perform the most difficult enterprises.

No prayer was so richly answered, as when Christ pleaded, "Let this cup pass from me." God said, no; but sent an angle to strengthen Him. Paul besought the Lord thrice, that his thorn in the flesh might be removed. God said, no; but, better than that, gave him grace to bear it.

***

The quality and extent of suffering depends not half so much on the exciting causes of it, as upon the nature of the faculty which suffers. It is the power of suffering that is inherent in any faculty that measures suffering, and not the magnitude of the aggression which is made outwardly. For there are many who will stand up and have their name battered as if they were but a target almost without suffering, the nature and quality of the love of praise in them being such that it is not wounded nor hurt; while there are others to whom the slightest disparagement is like a poisoned arrow, and rankles with exquisite suffering. There be men who all. their life long walk under an arch that rains down abuse, and care nothing for it; and there are others who, if touched, as it were, but by the point of a needle, are inoculated with incurable agony. It is the quality of a faculty that determines how much one suffers by it.

A stroke of a pound weight upon a bell two inches in diameter will give forth a certain amount of sound. Let the bell be of one hundred pounds weight, and the same stroke of one pound will more than quadruple the amount of aerial vibration. Let the bell be increased to a thousand pounds, and the same stroke will make the reverberations vaster, and cause them to roll yet further. Let it be a five or ten thousand pound weight bell, and that stroke that made a tingling on the small bell, makes a roar on this large one.

The very same quality that, being struck in a small being, produces a certain amount of susceptibility, being struck in a Being that is infinite, produces an infinitely greater experience, for feeling increases in the ratio of being.

* * *

God uses suffering as a whetstone, to make men sharp with. After you have made your knife sharp, your whetstone has served the purpose for which it was intended. But the ascetics seemed to think that if the whetstone was good to make men sharp, it was good to eat. And so they kept whetting till they ground off not only the edge, but the body of the blade.

* * *

No one has suffered enough until he is patient of suffering. "Made perfect through suffering!" Men stamped with this brand have God's mark on them.

* * *

Being drawn out and up is the business of this life. The ministry of suffering is to make us more courageous, and finally, under the economy of Divine help, to give us victory. Why the world is made so, you cannot answer, nor I, any more than you can tell why a daisy wasn't made like a dandelion, or a dandelion like a sunflower.

* * *

Pain and suffering in this world are God's merciful ministers to keep men in the road; they are the thorns of the hedge that save a man from toppling over the precipice on the other side, and the scratch is salvation.

* * *

I heard a conversation once, in the mountains. There was gold that had been wedged in among rocks, and had heard that gold was a wonderful thing for value and for beauty; and it was murmuring and saying, "Here I lie, and here I have lain for centuries; I am gold, and I hear stories of what gold is for value and for beauty and for power; but here I lie in darkness, crowded and hurt and crushed." The engineer says, "Well, if you want to come out and shine, you shall"; and there is joy in all the ledges until the powder explodes and they are torn to atoms, and thrown all round about. "Oh, oh, oh! this is what you have promised us—that we should have joy, liberty and beauty." They are trundled into wagons, lifted with the earth, and as the light dawns on them, they say, "Well, it may be alleviated a little, but this is a hard way to answer our aspiration". Then they are put down under the stamp, broken up with mallets, and at last ground into powder. They give up in despair. "If this is making us beautiful gold, we would rather go back to our ledges." Then the water takes out the rock, and the gold lies scattered, and it is then poured into a bath of quicksilver, that eats it all up; the gold has disappeared, the particles of quicksilver have got it all inside themselves. It is collected and carried out, and then, by heat, the quicksilver is dissipated, and the gold finds itself lying under the sky, pure — nearly; then it goes through the process of perfect purification, and, at last, it passes into the mint, where it takes the image and superscription of the government, wears the crown, carries the sceptre, and it is sought by all men, and is used in all places, and at last, through much tribulation, it enters into the kingdom of glory.

You do not know what is going on, you do not know all the meaning of your sorrow; God does. Do you suppose that the wool on the sheep's back knows what it is coming to when it is sheared? When it was scoured and washed and spun, and twisted of its life almost; when it went into the hateful bath of color; when it was put into the shuttle, and was thrust back and forth, back and forth, in the darkness, and out came the royal robe, it did not know what it started for; yet that is what it comes to — kings wear it. The flax in the field sighs to be made into the garment of the saints. All right. Pluck it up; rot it, put it under the brick, thread it, weave it, bleach it, purify it; and the saints may wear it now. It came to honor and glory through much suffering. "Who are these arrayed in white? These are they that have come out of great tribulation, and washed their robes and made them white in the blood of the Lamb." Suffering is God's guardian, guiding angel to those that will; it takes them up through the gate of trouble and trial to that land of perfectness and of everlasting peace.

* * *

God can suffer. I cannot worship a God that cannot suffer. It is not the suffering of ignominy, nor of physical pain, nor of the violation of law, but of sympathy. Love in its nature suffers.

* * *

It is not meant that we should go through this life acting as if the world were a life-boat, to be used merely for snatching as many folks from destruction as possible, and for taking them safely to heaven. This world is God's university or school, where men begin at zero, and are to unfold and come to manhood as the object of God's decrees and providence and grace, and of the common sense which God has given to us.

* * *

A true man is a force-bearer and a force-producer. I understand that when a man becomes a Christian he has higher ideals, larger conceptions of life here and of the life to come. The motives which are addressed to him from the bosom of God are an inspiration by which he becomes more, does more, longs for more, strives for more, gains more. Before, he lived a circumscribed life; but now he moves out the walls on every side because he needs more room. "Lengthen thy cords, and strengthen thy stakes," is the right text for a true man. He that is a Christian ought to be a hundred times larger in every way than he was before he became a Christian. Larger in every way? Yes; larger every way. What! larger in his passions? Yes; larger in his passions. His passions ought to be not only larger, but better and healthier. Pride ought to be stronger, only it ought to be in subjection to the law of love. It ought to be under the influence of love, auxiliary to higher things, and not an autocrat in its own right. Every part of a man's nature is to be built up, and is to be made subordinate to love. Anything that God thought it worth while to put in a man, from his toe to his eyebrow, from the crown of his head to the sole of his foot, is worthy of our consideration. He has not employed anything in the making of you that will not be needed for fuel.

He that is out of concord with those motions and throbs of the Divine Heart that send currents of light through the universe, is narrowing and dwarfing himself. He only is a full man who is a man in Christ Jesus.

Paul was the apostle of manhood — manhood in

Christ Jesus — He being both the model and the inspiration.

* * *

It is a good thing for a man, under a touching sermon, to experience pity; it is a better thing for a man never to be without it. It is a good thing, under song and speech, for men to be lifted up into the higher regions of aspiration; it is a better thing for a man to be there habitually, morning and night. It is a good thing for a man to have his heart touched with sympathy for his fellowmen; it is a better thing for a man's heart to abound in that quality. It is a good thing for a man to have, if he be thirsty, water that requires a great deal of labor to pump from the deep well; it is better that a man should have a spring that is so full that it gushes forth night and day out of the side of the hill. The piety that comes and goes is better than nothing — scarcely more than that; but the higher spiritual qualities of a man's nature that abide with him, and grow stronger and throw their roots deeper and take hold of life with more multiplied hands, are the qualities that constitute the true man.

* * *

Everybody can run down hill, but it takes a man to run up hill.

* * *

Christian manhood is higher than nationality.

A man is the grandest thing this side of God — should be, for he is the son of God, and the heir of immortality.

* * *

Whatever you wish to become, be it first in your manhood. Out of power develop trustworthiness. Out of energy develop various skill and competency. When you come to a point beyond which men do not want you, be content to stand there. Be content to stand where your avoirdupois puts you.

* * *

You should make your nobility consist in yourself — not in outward change; not in fictitious advancement, but in growing manhood, in a deeper consciousness, in a higher spirituality, in more manliness, in greater godliness, in more earnest striving after immortality.

* * *

Every man is an egg, and he ought to hatch his real mankind out of himself.

* * *

That which makes a man a better man is the best gift you can bestow on him. The best ointment which can be used to ordain the priest which is in a man, to ordain the God which is in a man, is to give him those sentiments and those affections, and to lift him to a higher level in life.

Every man that teaches himself to find the chief employments and enjoyments of his manhood lower than in his reason and moral sentiments and spiritual nature, has forsaken himself. Every man whose business is manual and physical, and who contents himself with that business, and feeds himself by nothing higher than that, is a creature that is spending his life forces lower than the level of true manhood. It is not a misfortune to be a mechanic; but it is a misfortune to be only a mechanic. It is not a misfortune to be a farmer, but it is a misfortune to be nothing but a farmer. It is not a misfortune to be a mariner, or a day-laborer; but the man that labors, working with his hands, and never thinks any higher than his work, is unfortunate. It is a misfortune for a man to have abandoned his manhood so that the operations of his mere physical frame shall satisfy him. All the upper realm of such a man's nature has been shut up. That which distinguishes him in the creation of his Father, that which gives him the right to say, "Our Father", is all disused. It is as if a man inheriting a magnificent palace, should shut up every one of the numerous apartments except the eating-room, and there live and feed.

***

If you have ever taken up a tree, and it was of any size, you know that a tree, which looks as though it were one stem growing out of the ground, is found to have, the moment you undertake to transplant it, five hundred stems under ground. Here is one great root, that you never knew anything about, by which it anchors itself; and there is another there; and there is another yonder. You take off the ground and cut away this root, and then shake the tree, and it stands just as though nothing had been done. You remove the earth and cut off that long anchor-root, and then you say, "Now it will come". No, it will not come. You dig again — a little impatient — with pick and spade, and you find that here is another root; and there is another root; and as you cut them off you say to yourself, "Will it never come up?" And you pull at it again. No, it will not come. And you get quite vexed, and you have an opportunity to get good natured again; for it does not come. By and by you say, "Well, I will see what is the matter"; and with the pick you strike under, and under, and under, until all at once, thump — you hit a great tap-root. That sheds new light on the subject. Here are all these surface roots that you have uncovered and cut; and finding that then the tree will not budge, you dig far under, and to your surprise find this tap-root; and with one powerful, sidelong blow you cut that off, and the tree falls over, and the victory is gained! Now, that is very much like transplanting a man. There are ever so many roots that hold him down. All the surface is full of them. They run great distances in every direction, dividing, bifurcating, twisting underneath stones, and around all sorts of obstructions. And when all these surface roots have been cut he is not half ready to transplant. You must dig under and under, till you come to the tap-root, that was far out of sight, and that nobody suspected, and cut that; and then you can transplant the man.

What do you suppose a crystal thinks when it is discovered in a rock by some prowling geologist or mineralogist? He knows that there is a wonderful crystal there; and so, with hammer and chisel, he smites off great chips from the rock, carefully watching on this side and on that, to discover the point where the crystal is to appear. And if the crystal is as ignorant as it ought to be, it murmurs because such violence is done to its surroundings; because its covering is being taken off; because its hiding-place is disclosed to the elements. But the rock is smitten right and left until the crystal comes out, when it shines in the rays of the sun, and is put to noble uses.

The manhood of man is shut up in that which is worse than a rock—in mud, composed of all manner of animalism; in filth of the appetites and passions; and it is this manhood that is being sought by providences that strike it here and there, cutting off this desire, and that pleasure; extinguishing this pride, and that vanity; and more and more bringing the man away from the lower and animal realm, to a higher region, where he sees the lustre of those virtues which bring him into affinity, and which will finally bring him into contact, with God.

Aspire, find out the source of your Christ-life, and grow in grace. Knowledge comes from likeness. Put on Jesus Christ as a garment. Eat Him as bread; drink Him as wine, or the water of life. Be Christ; not in the sphere of the Infinite, but in the sphere of your own personality. Then, knowing Him, give forth the word of life and the light of life, that men, seeing you, may glorify your Father which is in heaven.

Every true man is like the true Christ that is in him. There is something of the earth with which he treads upon the ground and with which he deals with things as they are; there are also high celestial faculties that commune with God and with the invisible realm; and the perfect character is the one which combines them both.

There are many fine natures hidden under coarse forms. Powerful impressions are produced on many who cannot resolve them into ideas, and still less fashion them to words. Along the furrow, by the workbench, in the chamber, or in the kitchen, have been thousands silently plying the unknown with as solemn an earnestness as that of those who write books to prove how little man can know of the Unknowable.

When you cry out for God, he will cry out for you. There was never a heart homesick for heaven, that heaven was not homesick for it. Never did a soul long for God, that God did not long for that soul.

Have you ever been among the songsters on the edge of a forest in June, and heard the warblers singing, and the sparrows chirping, and the blue-birds' exquisite little lady-note? If, during a chorus of birds' voices, a hawk in the air, so high as not to throw a shadow on the ground, should but once scream, every little voice would be hushed. One note up there is enough to put to silence five hundred notes down here. So it is in the human soul. Men have all manner of ecstacies; but let there be one hawk-note struck, and it will put all these ecstasies and joys to flight.

There are multitudes that are like my Wisteria — a plant of the loveliest habit, which you shall see in the early spring abundantly, in the cities and in the country. When transplanted it is very apt to be obstinate and to refuse to grow. I planted it early, and I got a little dwarf, stumpy vine, tree-like, not two feet high. I waited one year, two years, three years, four years, until I got out of all patience with it, and I said to the gardener, "Take it up; throw it away". He took it up, but not to throw it away. He planted it in a more favorable corner, where something happened, I know not what, in the mystery of nature, and the very next year it broke its bonds and sent up its vine, and clasped and clambered and covered all the end of the house, and ran up on to the adjacent trees, and filled the whole air with its perfume and with the beauty of its blossom. Multitudes of men there are just like it, living so near the ground, and without any aspiration, that they never know what they are, in themselves, and to what their possibilities lead up — never.

Vanity makes us wish to be superior to others, moral aspiration to be superior to ourselves.

While the practical is an indispensable part of the mind, that life in the soul which never has an exponent of words or deeds, is the noblest. The heroism, the enthusiasms, the silent thought and holy aspirations, God regards as the best part of the soul.

True aspiration is not to wish to be different from what God has made us, but to be able to develop all that He has put into us.

* * *

As a lake, when all the streams have emptied their fulness into it, when first it sees the ray and feels the warmth of the sun, begins to rise toward it in mists and exhalations, so the heart filled with all that earth can supply, when first it lies consciously in the presence of God, aspires toward him, sets with all its tides in that direction.

* * *

What we call yearning is the heart of God drawing us heavenward.

* * *

Even the poor mute root in the cellar, that lies all winter long — the turnip, or the potato — dead, yet knows when April and May come, knows that there is a sun out-side, and begins to sprout, and finds its way, growing in the dark with long, long vines; and if there be a slit or a crack, it will work toward the light; and shall not I, that am no root nor vegetable, no matter through what winters, find my way toward the great Center of warmth and light? If there is summer in heaven I will find it. Though I be plunged into the depths of hell, I long for such a God as is manifest by Jesus Christ; and I will find Him. I shall see Him for myself, and not another for me. I shall be like him yet, though it may be myriads of ages hence.

※※※

The whole man, in orderly succession, unfolds through successive stages. The kingdom of God is the highest stage. That is the blossom of all the rest. We are made perfect men in Christ Jesus. Before that time we are raw, unripe, undeveloped, undisclosed; we are plants that grow in a clime so far north that the summer is not warm enough nor long enough to show what they are in their higher development.

※※※

The growth of the Church is not by the numbers that are in it, but by the graces, the beauty of holiness, the variety and ripeness of Christian feeling character. These are signs of growth. Whatever tends to make men, looking upon you, revere you, esteem you, love you, whatever lifts their conception of your spiritual excellence, gives strength to the Church.

※※※

Many persons boil themselves down to a kind of molasses goodness. It is not such goodness as there is in the live peach, in the luscious apple, or in the delicious pear. It is not such goodness as has in it the power and the sharpness which belong to a combination of acid and sweet. It is inspirated goodness. It is partial goodness, joined to feebleness, caution, fear.

*

How many persons are in the world as flies that have been caught in some sweet liquid, that have got out at last upon the side of the cup, drabbled, and crawl up slowly, buzzing a little to clear their wings! Just such Christians I have seen, creeping up the side of churches, soul-poor, imperfect, without inspiration, and drabbled. If it must needs be so, that is better than nothing; it is better than to die without moral rebound; but this is not the whole career. You are called to manliness, and to strength, and to variety, and to development. You are called to an allsidedness in Christian life.

*

To avoid evil is good only so far as it impels you to perform the right; only so far as it leads you to grow in the direction of true manliness.

What would you account that husbandry to be worth which succeeded only in keeping down weeds? A man goes on ploughing and ploughing, harrowing and harrowing, hoeing and hoeing; and he rejoices, as July comes on, saying, "There is not a weed on my farm — not a weed". Round and round he goes, looking into every corner, and under every hedge, to spy out any weeds that may have been left; and he says, "Not one weed shall grow on this farm". But where is thy corn, O farmer? "I have no corn." Where is thy wheat? "I have no wheat." Where are thy fruits? "I have no fruits." What hast thou? "No weeds!"

How many there are who are circumspect, and are in earnest, not only, but whose whole care is not to speak a wrong word, nor speak a word in the wrong place! The result is, that they succeed in doing nothing. Their life is comparatively rapid and void, because they have adapted themselves and confined themselves to one single element. They violate no propriety, but they are living negative instead of positive lives.

Any man that has ceased to grow is waiting for his undertaker; and the longer he has to wait the greater is the pity for everybody about him; for the fruitfulness of benefiting life goes with this onward movement—this enlargement which we call growth.

No man has a right to be a puddle. Every man is bound to have a life that flows and cleanses itself by its own activity. No man has a right to rust. Every man is bound to keep his faculties bright by incessant use. No man has a right to stand paralyzed. Every man is bound to grow. The Divine conception is transfer of power from the animal to the spiritual man, the development in the spiritual man of the highest ideals; and then the strife and struggle of life is to lift one's self up through every stage of education until he reaches that highest form of intellectual and moral development—perfect manhood, the perfect man in Christ Jesus.

* * *

The order of Christian development is much like the kindling of a fire. When a man has been brought up about right by his parents, indoctrinated in and trained to Christian morality, and steadily and gradually made to raise the standard of his convictions higher and higher, he is like kindling prepared in a fire-place, with light wood and dry fuel; and when religion just touches a match to it, it blazes right up at once.

But where men are very ignorant and very gross, religion is much like kindling a fire in old Connecticut when I was a boy. Every night I lugged in snow-clad logs of green oak, and such material for kindling as I could manage to get; and coming down in the morning, every finger numb, and shivering all over in those great winters of Connecticut—a little State, but big winters—and with but a few coals gathered, the making of the fire was a very artistic and delicate process. The match kindled the shaving, and the shaving kindled the splinter, and the stick had to be kindled by the splinter—just a light, dry splinter, the smallest wood that I could get—and then, when the fire had begun to get hold, volumes of blue smoke rolled up the chimney—what I didn't breathe. A little more, and a little more fuel, had statedly to be put on, until by and by a smudgy faint flame began to appear, and then, with bellows in hand, I applied the means of the gospel. There is a contest, and it is doubtful which will conquer; but at length the flame makes way, and the smoke grows thinner, and the flame becomes broader, until by and by it has penetrated the whole mass, and the log sings at each end, expelling the sap by the growing flame, and, at length, the light blazes in all of the chimneys, and sends back the children that huddled around it at first, and the whole room is full of light and red heat. The fire is kindled, and the glory of it is felt in the whole house.

That is just about the way some men come from a state of sinfulness to a state of grace. It is pretty hard kindling them, they are pretty tough, and they are full of sap, and they are covered with habits of snow and ice, and the first ideas they get of religion are very faint ones; and they fight with old passions and appetites; but by the blowing of the gospel continuously, you can keep it going; and if by faith and patience you continue it long enough, the whole soul begins to be on fire, and when it is once on fire the the light and warmth pervade the whole dwelling.

All true religious growth is toward sweetness. Mildness and sweetness are the characteristics of ripeness.

If, therefore, you find that one is more stringent, more sharp, more consciously greedy as he grows in Christian life, you may be sure that he took the wrong shoot. He is not growing the right way.

There are a great many men like one of my roses. I bought a *Gloire de Dijon*. It was said to be one of the few ever-blooming roses. It was grafted on a mannetti stalk—a kind of dog-rose, a rampant and enormous grower, and a very good stalk to graft fine roses on. I planted it. It throve the first part of the summer, and the last part of the summer it grew with great vigor; and I quite gloried, when the next spring came, in my *Gloire de Dijon*. It had wood enough to make twenty such roses as these finer varieties usually have; and I was in the amplitude of triumph. I said, "My soil suits it exactly in this climate, and I will write an article for the *Monthly Gardener*, and tell what luck I have had with it." So I waited and waited, and waited till it blossomed; and behold! it was one of those worthless, quarter-of-a-dollar, single-blossomed roses. And when I came to examine it, I found that it was grafted, and that there was a little bit of a graft down near the ground, and that it was the mannetti sprout that had grown to such a prodigious size.

Now I have seen a great many people converted, in whom the conversion did not grow, but the old nature did. A man may be a Christian, you know, in a spot; and growth in that spot should be such as to keep down nature. The whole power of the root should be thrown into the new scion, which should make the stem and the top. If, therefore, you see a man that is sharp, and full of thorns, you may be sure that it is a mannetti stalk that is growing, and not a *Gloire de Dijon* — nor a *Gloire de Jerusalem*, either! It is nature, and not grace. For just as sure as God is love, so sure they that are His children, and that are growing according to the new nature in Christ Jesus, are growing toward gentleness and sweetness, and easy-to-be-entreatedness. They are full of love, and the fruits of love. An eminent development in grace is an eminent development toward gentleness and sweetness and agreeableness.

Your trying and waiting are not in vain, as you will see by and by. There is another life besides this, which you are going to live in. What you are doing here you will not know till you get there.

When we come into the fullness of knowledge in the presence of God, all that we know on earth will seem to us like child-shadows. In the grandeur of the final development, all the twilight knowledge that we have in this world shall seem to flit away in the rising sun itself.

When I see in the spring the trees full of bud and

ready to bloom in the orchard, I hear complaint in the outside green coating of the bud, that has wrapped it up like an overcoat, and carried it through the winter. As the balmy atmosphere begins to expand the bud, I hear the sepal mourn and say, "Alas, alas! I am being expelled and pushed down; the hinges are breaking off, I have got to drop." And go it does in some high wind; but it goes in order that the blossom may live. Then after a little while I hear the blossom say, "I have got to fall"—and fall it does, to the ground, in order that the fruit may spring forth. And when men mourn because they are losing this faculty and that faculty, they forget that they are failing here in order that glorious virtues and perfect holiness may emerge to ripen forever in heaven. Yes, it is a glorions thing to believe in a life to come. This is what I call the true practical theology of human life.

We do not make the first and last experiment here. We are not going to waste the whole of this life, dying at death and going out into darkness. We shall live again, and live under better influences. This is, or ought to be, a consolation to those who have no opportunities here which are fitting to their nature.

I cannot be one of those who think that this world is all there is of the manifestation of the glory of God.

I would sooner think that all the majestic pines that frown from the ridges of California are contained in a seed no bigger than a pea. That seed has to be planted, and it must develop. This world, with its poverty, with its ignorance, with its grinding customs — is that all there is? Much as there is of God made manifest in this world — is it all? God forbid that I should impoverish the conception of His great providence by limiting it to the possibilities of this life.

This glorious vision, this hope and everlasting surety of the future, how shallow were life without it, and how deep beyond all fathoming with it! The threads that broke in the loom here shall be taken up there. The veins of gold that penetrate this mighty mountain of Time and Earth, shall then have forsaken the rock and dirt, and shine in a sevenfold purity. All those wrongly estranged and separated; and all who, with great hearts, seeking good for men, do yet fall out and contend; and all they who bear about hearts of earnest purpose, longing to love, and to do, but hindered and baulked, and made to carry hidden fire in their souls that warms no one, but only burns the censor; and all they who are united for mutual discomfort; and all who are separated that should have walked together; and all that inwardly or outwardly live in a dream all their days, longing for the dawn and the waking — to all such how blessed is the dawn of the Resurrection! The stone is rolled away, and angels sit upon it; and all who go groping toward the grave to search for that which is lost, shall hear their voices teaching them that Heaven harvests and keeps whatever of good the earth loses.

※※

When God sends wealth to bless men, he sends it gradually, like a gentle rain.

※※

There are two things about riches — one is to catch them, another is to hold them. I have seen many a man get money as a man catches a bird. He has the bird safe till he goes to put it into the cage, but when he opens his hand to put it in, out and off it flies. So the riches of men take to themselves wings and fly away.

※※

That prosperity which grows like the mushroom is as poisonous as the mushroom.

※※

Few men are destroyed, but many destroy themselves.

※※

If a man, being a mineralogist, has a finer crystal than anybody else, he rather glories in it, and says, "You ought to see mine". If a man is a gardener, and has finer roses than anybody else, he glories in them. He may go to his neighbor's garden, and praise the flowers that he sees there; but he says, "I should like to have you come over and see my roses". And he shows them with pride. Nobody shuts his own garden-gate when he goes to see his neighbor's garden. He carries his own with him. Men glory in such outward things; but how many glory in those diamonds, those sapphires — those precious stones which all the world recognize as the finest graces of the soul? How many men glory because they have the true, universal, Christian benevolence of love? Who can say, "I am rich — I know that; I am honored — I know that; I have a wide sweep of influence, authority, power — I know that; but all these things are merely external; I might as well glory in my clothes as to glory in them. I thank God, however, that I have one occasion for pride, in that I am filled with the love that God is filled with. I value myself on that account?"

No man will stand long in any security in his riches, or with any great comfort in his luxuries, who does not make his riches serve the wants of common humanity. Men are not to be heroic, even in the court of Mammon, by the magnitude of their riches, but by the uses of them. Men are not to be laureled and crowned by their profligate expenditure, by their wanton exhibition of what their wealth will enable them to do, by their attempting to gild and garnish and glorify all the lower, all the more sensuous elements in human life, because they have the money. Men who are to have large properties are coming rapidly under the responsibility of using them for the public welfare, and not alone for their own selfishness. The man that stands to-day upon a pedestal simply because he is rich, will in another fifty years stand in the pillory if he does not make his riches serve mankind.

When a man wants more money than he can use, he wants too much.

Let no man glory in his riches unless they are riches which are the certificate of God's providence that they have been men in the earning of them — that their external riches represent internal worth.

The man who gets wealth legitimately is usually himself built up in inward riches fully as much as he builds up his estate in outward wealth. It is a good thing that men have to work long and hard, because long and hard work prepares a man for the use and for the larger enjoyment of riches, by and by, when he has attained it. Men that come to riches suddenly are usually either very much injured or entirely destroyed by it, simply because they have not been trained to use it. They do not know what to do with it, and it does what it pleases with them.

* * *

Have a deposit on earth, if you must or can; but let your chief banking be in heaven. Lay up your treasure there. That which you pride yourself on, which is your main reliance, which is the substance of your life and pleasure—let that be heavenly treasure, moral quality.

* * *

Geologists sometimes find toads sealed up in rocks. They crept in during the formation periods, and deposits closed the orifice through which they entered. There they remain, in long darkness and toad stupidity, till some chance blast or stroke sets them free. And there are many rich men sealed up in mountains of gold in the same way. If, in the midst of some convulsion in the community, one of these mountains is overturned, something crawls out into life which is called a man!

* * *

The power of wealth is what it can do for humanity. If it can make you happier, if it gives you more exalted leisure, more knowledge, or opportunities for it; if it enables you to bring up your family in a wider and better sphere; if it overflows, and produces in your town and neighborhood public benefaction; if you are the headwaters of the stream, as it were, that waters the city of God in this world, blessed is your wealth, and you, that you are permitted to exercise it in such a way. But wealth unused is wealth that is dead. Unused wealth is of no more use to a community than are the men that lie in mausoleums a thousand years old — the dust of the sepulcher. Money is like powder. It has no power until it is set off.

We think, we plan, we build, we reach out for things, as if it were forever, and as if all that we are to enjoy must now speedily be had; and so we fill each day striving to heap up its enjoyments, and forgetting, as the shadows fall and grow longer, that this is not our home; that this is not our true life; that we belong to the beyond, and are on our way thither; and that that which is true strength and true riches does not lie in outward estate, nor in the thoughts of men respecting us, nor in our own thoughts of ourselves.

A man is not to be known by how much money he has, but by what money is worth to him. You must put your hand into a man's heart to find out how much he is worth, not into his pocket.

A geode is a rude, rough stone that you will find in

the fields — ragged, coarse and homely; yet, when it is selected by the expert eye of the mineralogist, and is broken open, its chamber is one mass of beautiful crystals, beautiful whether white or amethystine. And thus many of the texts in Scripture are geodes; the outward rind, as it were, not being particularly handsome, but the inwardness of them being exquisite.

The Bible is on the side of the workingmen. It is on the side of the slave. It is on the side of men that are under hard governments. It is on the side of men that are sick and that have failed under the harness of life. It is on the side of men whose consciences roar out at them like enraged lions; on the side of sinful, suffering humanity; and a book like that is not going to be kicked over by ridicule, nor disposed of by angry scholarship, nor by the impudent superiority of men. It is the people's book; a book of life, that carries in its heart the very element of life for the human race.

The Bible is the only book that develops God in human conditions, that cheers the end of life, opening the doors of immortality; the only book, that, from beginning to end, has sympathy with the poor and weak and struggling — the sorrowful, the sinful. All theories of the nature of the sun may be assailed, but the sun shines on and cares naught for them. All theories respecting the history and structure of the Bible may be mooted and disputed; but there it is, a book whose fruits rise higher, smell sweeter, taste more flavorsome, inspire more health, than any or all others that have been produced upon the plane of human life.

The Bible is not a book written as John Milton wrote "Paradise Lost", nor is it a book written as a man writes a history. It is not a book; it is a series of books, with intervals of hundreds of years between. It is the record of the progress of the human race in their development into the Divine idea through the medium of right-living. It is the serial history of the construction of the noblest elements that belong to human consciousness.

The Old Testament was a book of time. The New is a book of Eternity. The Old Testament taught religion for its benefits in this world — the New Testament for its benefits in the world to come. It is very fitting, therefore, that they should be joined together to make one book. The Old Testament attempted to bring men into harmony with natural laws. The New Testament seeks to harmonize men with spiritual laws. The Old Testament, in short, lay within the horizon of this world; the New Testament lies beyond the horizon of time and the world.

**

What wonder that the Bible is, in its undertones, a requiem? What wonder that every form of sorrow and suffering finds a voice somewhere between the beginning and the end of the record? And what wonder that no philosophy and no infidelity can ever tear this book from the hands of men that once have received it, because it is in such intimate fellowship with that condition which runs through the world of weakness and sorrow and suffering which need sympathy, recognition and consolation? It is a book for the poor, it is a book for the weak, it is a book for all sufferers; for while it recognizes their suffering it holds over all the radiant promise of God's sympathy, and God's succor, and the hope of that immortality which will make everything straight that is crooked and everything harmonious that is at discord here.

The Bible is first and last simply a book that teaches the art and science of right living. That is the Bible. It is a chart, a map. The shipmaster going out of the port of New York has the whole course between here and Liverpool laid down, across the depths of the sea. But he does not understand hydraulics, nor the elements of water. He does not understand the geological questions connected with the sand — where it came from. There is a myriad of phenomena day and night that belong to the ocean, and with which more or less he is concerned, but what he wants is this: "What is the course by which I shall steer; what are the currents, where are the sands, and where the dangerous rocks." He steers by that chart and comes safely to his harbor.

The New Testament is as full of light as it is of consolation. Joy and hope flash through every page of it. There never was so unmorbid a book. There was never a book that was keyed so high, and that so maintained itself through all its parts up to the grand culmination of the apocalyptic vision, where you see the drama of human life, its conflicts, its wails, its disasters, its amazing triumphs, its victories, and its disclosures into the other life.

The Bible is a man-building book. If you want to know how to build a good house, you go to an architect and get a plan for it. Every stone will then come to its place, each to its fellow; the timber will be upon the wall, and each beam will be found in its appointed place, no matter whether men understand, no matter whether the timber is oak or pine or hemlock or beech or maple, or anything else. He may not understand vegetable physiology, but there is the plan, and the house will be completed if the plan has been skillfully drawn.

The word of God is a well-drawn plan for human life. Let a man, without attempting to probe the heavens or make the circuit and swing of the eternities, see what is right for him and what is wrong for him. Let him build him a character upon this plan of the great Architect, and no man will fail.

A man does not have music in his house because he has all Beethoven's symphonies there in a book shut up. Men think they have a good deal of gospel because they have a good many Bibles; but a dead Bible and a dead music book are just alike. While the score has every information for the performer, it has no intrinsic value — it is not music. Merely put to the harp, or to the organ, a hand that knows where the music is, and how to bring it out, and the music comes.

God does not live in a book. Man does not live in a book. Love, Faith, Joy, Hope do not, cannot live in a book. For the living truth we must go outside of the Bible, which is but to religion what a Botany is to gardens, meadows, and all their flowers! I feel as if some sort of positive relationship existed between me and every living thing. A spice bush, a clump of wild azaleas, a bed of trailing arbutus, a patch of eyebrights, a log covered with green moss — these all seem to be of my family kin. The spiders, too, the crickets, the field-mice, and all the swarms of birds; the worm — that as a child I was taught to abhor — are of God's family and mine. Since I accepted the New Testament, all the world has become my Bible. My Saviour is everywhere — in the book, and out of the book. I see him in Nature, in human life, in my own experience as well as in the recorded fragments of His own history. I live in a Bible. But it is an unbound book! It is wider than that I can reach its bounds. It is enough for me that I believe when it is said, "All things were made by Him, and without Him was not anything made that was made".

Many passages of the Scripture are like wayside flowers; though transcendently beautiful in themselves, they remain unnoticed, because all our life long we have been accustomed to see without examining them closely. Or they are like the treasures of art upon the walls of some old convent; overlaid with mould, and dust, and grime, they have been before our eyes all our days without being recognized in their resplendent excellence.

The Bible gives the only grand ideal of manhood known to literature. Great qualities have been praised by pagans, but there has never been in any literature that I know of anything more than dashes at the truth. From the remotest and darkest periods, there has come to us through the Bible the truth that Love is the organizing center of human character, the only quality to which all other elements of the mind will submit; the natural, organic force, which develops order and harmony. It is more than a descant on the beauty and sweetness of personal affection. The Bible reveals Love as the Universal Law of Humanity. Nor has this been without its commentary, in the fact that within the last two thousand years men have been growing up into the stature and spirit of Jesus Christ, approximately realizing this otherwise ideal conception of what man may become.

It is not a mere ideal — this book. It is a living book, shooting out rays of light and heat into all the world. It is clothed at this hour with the associations of myriads of hearts who discover in it the secret of their own lives. It is the seed-bed of all that is fine, all that is sweet, all that is strong, all that is aspiring and ennobling in the highest human character and conduct. Every morning the sun rolls over fields, forests, flowers and fruits, which itself has created. The Sun of Righteousness so shines in the Bible. It moves among men netted all over with the sweetest and tenderest emotions of the human soul, which itself has created as the revelation and voice of God. He who knows only the print and the type of the book, knows only a painted sun. What the Bible is, can be remotely appreciated only by those who can perceive what are its fruits. Like a cloud in summer, every drop brings forth a flower.

* * *

The Bible is inspired of God. We are to bear in mind that his inspiration — the in-breathing of His power, of His thought, of His will — is the cause of everything in the universe. The Bible, as I look upon it, is the record in part of what the influence of God's Spirit moving on human consciousness has brought to pass along the course of one national history. It is the record in a particular line, of the effect of that universal and continuous action of the Divine mind on the human mind, that has raised man from the lowest barbaric depths, step by step, unfolding moralities, social life, all graces, all affections, all reason, all the treasures of moral nature, and all spiritualities. It is the human race that has been inspired; and the Bible in every part of it was lived first, and the record of it made afterward. As a great poet never originates, but only throws into masterful forms the sum of all the thoughts and feelings that exist down to his time; as Shakespeare did not create his characters, but saw them, and with genius had the power to gather them together in groups and unfold them, not as anything that was new, but as that which was existing, though incoherent, dispersed, inorganic; so, the race itself was inspired to growth, and lived until some results of experience had become widespread and vaguely recognized. The time came when a man of large nature, feeling more sensitively the impulse of the Divine inspiration, was able to gather, to fix, and give out as a truth these unorganized elements — never, perhaps, before put into regular form, and spoken. They were found out to be real and authoritative before he declared it. Many good things in civil laws are, comparatively speaking, laws by public sentiment before they become authoritative laws by legislative enactment. So there are myriads of truths that are unfolded in action and in fact, long before authority is given them by anybody that declares them, crying, "Thus saith the Lord!" God does say so; but he says so first through the findings-out, through the trials, the failures and mistakes, the successes and ascertainments, of actual human experience. And so the Word of God is the record along one line of a grand experiment, namely, the high development of men from the lowest point of possible human existence through the experience of human life.

* * *

No wheat can grow without the straw, but when the straw has brought it forth, both straw and stubble perish. The wheat does not; it contains the germ of life within itself. And there are a thousand things which were employed of God's providence in the development of the truths of His word, which things are not to be held on to. They at length become the bark, and even moss on the bark, and not anything that is helpful.

***

While evolution is certain to oblige theology to reconstruct its system, it will take nothing away from the grounds of true religion. It will strip off Saul's unmanageable armor from David, to give him greater power over the giant. Simple religion is the unfolding of the best nature of man toward God, and man has been hindered and embittered by the outrageous complexity of unbearable systems of theology that have existed. If you can change theology, you will emancipate religion; yet men continually confound the two terms — religion and theology. They are not alike. Religion is the condition of a man's nature as toward God and toward his fellowmen. That is religion — love that breeds truth, love that breeds justice, love that breeds harmonies of intimacy and intercommunication, love that breeds duty, love that breeds conscience, love that carries in its hand the scepter of pain, not to destroy and to torment, but to teach and to save. Religion is that state of mind in which a man is related by his emotions, and through his emotions by his will and conduct, to God and to the proper performance of duty in this world. Theology is the philosophy of God, of divine government, and of human nature. The philosophy of these may be one thing; the reality of them may be another and totally different one. Though intimately connected, they are not all the same. Theology is a science; religion, an art.

*
* *

Science does not destroy the doctrine of human sinfulness; it explains it, it defines it, it throws a clearer light upon it. The old doctrine of sin, which it seems to me no man of moral feeling could allow himself to stand on for an hour or a moment, was that the human race born of their progenitors fell with them, and that the curse of God rested upon the whole human posterity, and that therefore all men by reason of their connection with Adam, are born without original righteousness, without true holiness and without communion with God. They were born without righteousness and holiness and communion with God, and they were born without everything else, too; they were born with feet that could not walk, and with hands that could not handle, and with eyes that could not see, and with ears that could not hear; they were born without arithmetic, without grammar; they were born without anything but potential power, with the capacity to come to these things by the process of unfolding, and when men say the whole human family is born without righteousness, of course it is; that is a thing that belongs to development and to conscious volition later on. Now what is sin? How would it be defined from the standpoint of sense if you accept the doctrine of Evolution, that if man was not actually developed from the animal, he was so near to him that he was substantially an animal in his savage state? But admit for the moment that man was primarily an animal, born and developed from his congeners into a higher state; that there was superinduced upon him a moral element, a spiritual element, a rational element. The animal man was first in order, and too often in strength, in the primitive day, in the early day of every man. And sin lies in the conflict between the upper and the under man. If you want to see the doctrine stated in its most cogent form, read the seventh chapter of Romans, where the conflict is not between a man before he is converted, and after he is converted, but between the man animal and the man moral and spiritual; where he thinks the highest things, and would fain do the highest things, but is pulled down and dragged under perpetually by the forces of his animal body. Sin is the remainder, as it were, of the conflict between man moral and spiritual and man animal and so far degraded. And this gives not simply a rational explanation that every man's reason can perceive; but it takes away the idea from the administration of God that men were cursed in their birth without any fault of their own, and that they were being punished throughout all ages in this world on account of a sin that they never committed. They have had no part or lot in their great-forefather's temptation and fall, but they have had to have their dividend in that everlasting, increasing and ever-rolling damnation that came to them in consequence of it.

Sounds are very impressive, but silence is far more so; and to me no silence is like that of universal sunlight. Out of its stillness come all the energies which awaken life upon the globe. It is father of the forest and the field. It creates the currents of the ocean and the storms of the air, and yet the sunlight itself is forever tranquil. It is to me the most impressive feature of the world. It is that symbol which most nearly represents the universality of God, the energy and fruitfulness of Divine power and its modesty, as well.

None in life sing so sweetly as they who, like the wood-thrush, sit on the twilight edge of solitude and sing to men who pass by in the sunlight outside.

It is solitude that gives zest to society, and goodly company it is that prepares you for the joys of solitude. Alone-ness is to social life what rests are in music. Sounds following silence are always sweetest.

How full the universe is! And yet it does not make any noise. It is a universe of silence. Silence is God's chamber hinted at even in Nature. Nothing is stiller than the collection of those moist drops that are preparing the way for a storm. Though it comes bellowing down from the recesses of the heavens, all its energy was gathered in perfect silence. That which is going on to make the summer fruitful goes on in silence. A million roots are pumping, and no man hears the pumping. A million roots are exuding forms, but there is no sound of the hammer or of the chisel. All is silence. The great work of the physical creation is steadily unfolding in silence. How full is the heaven around us, above us, and beyond us! But to our hearing there are no voices, there is no sound, there is only silence. It is not less populus, nor less active; but more so.

There ought to be but one key to a man's privacy, and that is in his own hands; but the devil has given everybody a key to it, and everybody goes in and out and filches whatever he pleases.

I know that there remaineth a rest for the people of God. Storms drive us toward it. The thunder and crash of earthly discordance are, after all, but the background on which there shall be the sweet melodies of the heavenly life.

Oh! let us not be forever on the storm-washed shore. Let us not be forever swept and rocked by the winds. May we at last find that land where there are no storms; where is settled peace; from which we behold the battlement afar off, where are wafted snatches of that blessed song which we, too, ere long, shall sing. And we pray that we may gird up our loins, make a new crown of faith, and again press upward and forward, undiscouraged, undismayed, not daunted by suffering, nor by sorrow, nor by any evil that shall come upon us. Holding all our life subject to Thy will, may we take or part with whatever is best. May we bear our burdens, or find them rolling off, as pleases Thee; so that in all things our will and Thine shall be one and inseparable.

* * *

Do you know what emphasis there is in the words — When we shall see Him as He is? The things that are past will grow dim and die away. They will be taper-lights, at most. But the glory, the majesty, the magnitude, the bounty, the sweetness, the transcendent riches of the Divine Heart, will fill every soul that beholds God as He is. Silence will first reign and then rapture will break forth from each heart, and heaven will resound with shouts of the redeemed. No man can learn here what it will be to feel the full power of the goodness and love and mercy of the heart of God that has cleansed his. But we are all traveling toward that great tropical Center.

This world is the workshop of heaven. There we

shall see the consummation of that which we see but feebly and understand but partially. The law of suffering runs on beyond, I believe, in multitudes of cases, although the final consummation is perfect and increscent joy and happiness. Many there are on earth who see no outcome; they are underfoot, they are out of place; suffering seems not only to bring to them no relief and no inspiration, and no help and no hope, but it seems never to have declared its real nature to their surroundings or to their generations. Oh! there will be a land where these things will be known; there will be an interpretation to every pang and to every tear and to every crushing sorrow; and as for those who suffer for a noble cause, who suffer for children, who suffer for those who have no parents, who suffer for the community, though they are accounted unworthy, and are cast out by the community, though they be crushed out of life and hope, and go mourning all the days of their lives, there is a reckoning — that is to say, there is to be an unfolding of the reasons of their suffering, and the results of it, which do not by any means all appear upon this mortal sphere and in this limited life — it is to be made known.

Here all things do change. Our honors blossom and fade; and riches make to themselves wings and fly away. Our affections we invest in dying men; and the grave is the house for all human creatures. Thither we bear our children and companions and laborers that have worked together with us in the vineyard; and everything runs to ceaseless change in this life, so brief, so full of vanity. But there is a rest that doth not change. It remains. It waits. None can dispossess us of it. No bankruptcy shall enter into our estate to reach us there. Nothing shall disturb us in that peaceful abode. Though the storm may blow, we have a refuge. Though the sea may cast up mire and dirt, we have a faith that shall enter within the veil — a sure anchor, steadfast and abiding. The hereafter comforts the hitherward.

Teach us the grand life of love; prepare us to go up, but let us not go till we can speak its language; prepare us to go up hearing afar off the chant, the anthem of love. With feeble murmuring voice we call to Thee, "We are coming". We hear Thee shout from the battlements, "Come, come, come all, and take of the water and live freely". Parched and thirsty, and scarcely articulating, we say, "Lord, we are coming". Our children come and meet us, our venerable parents are there, the gates are flung open, the great procession pours forth; we have an exceeding abundant entrance ministered unto us as we come to the kingdom of love, and when we shall enter in and behold Thee, for the moment we shall forget all other things to cast ourselves down in Thy presence, to love Thee and adore Thee, and as the sun gives all the beauty that there is in flower and tree, or earth or sky, so it shall be Thyself that shall give the love, the fatherhood, the motherhood, the brotherhood, the childhood — everything, more beautiful because it will shine in the radiance of Thy love.

*　*　*

Make this life as the very verge of the great life beyond; and though in the stillest hour we can hear nothing, O, grant that by faith we may see and hear much. As men that live far away from the sea hear the roar of the waves upon the shore, so may we hear the praise that beats upon the shores of the other life, where Thou hast gathered multitudes that no man can number; where their joy mounts higher than our summer; where everything blooms and everything rejoices. As we hear it, may we rejoice that we are drawing nearer to it, and be ashamed that our voices are so poorly constituted to join in that praise with which Thou art surrounded.

*　*　*

Teach us all to be patient while we are bearing burdens And as we find our limitations, as one by one the signs of the coming departure are made known to us, grant that we may rejoice to see the tokens of the coming of the Son of man. As they that have dwelt long in the wilderness at last rejoicingly begin to take down the tent, and prepare to go home, so may we be homesick for heaven. And when one and another of the things that belong to life, when one and another of the parts of this tabernacle are being taken down, grant that we may turn with unspeakable joy, and see the light increasing, the morning coming, the victory rending the sky. And so may we live that at last death itself shall be the consummation of triumph. May we go to glory, and from glory to glory, until we stand in Zion and before God.

* * *

If he that gives a cup of cold water to a little child in the name of Christ shall not fail of his reward, how much less he that opens springs in the desert, that strikes the rocks in the mountains so that they gush forth, that digs wells from which men through generations can drink. Do the little that you can; do more if you can; and when at last you return with joy upon your head to enter in at the gate, there shall throng forth from it so many that you cannot count them, of those who were refreshed in the hours of sorrow and weariness of the way by your labor, and they shall come with rosy hand and joyful lip to greet you and to bring you before the throne of the Saviour. And when once you shall have beheld that loving, adorable face, though you have suffered on the cross, though you had wilted in the dungeon, though you had been broken on the rack, though you had reached Him through the fires of martyrdom — one look will be more, a thousand times more, than all the suffering. And to hear Him say, "Well done" — not all the music that time has known, not all the coronets that power has worn, not all the treasures of the earth, nor all the bounties of the summer with all its sun, can compare for one single moment with the rapture that will thrill through the heart of one who is saved — safe, welcomed, forever and ever accepted.

Life is but the beginning of things, and has not been so far unfolded as yet that we can see from the things in us and around us what sorrow does, nor what repentance does, nor what stumbling does, nor what oppressions and wrongs do. There is to be a time of disclosure, when the end shall have come, and the experiment of unnumbered centuries shall have been wrought out, and we shall all have gone from hence, and become airy spectators of the closing work in the other life. God knows that then the whole interior history of man and providence and experience will declare, "God is good, and the end crowns the beginning and the whole work".

I cast into the ground the seed of the magnolia; the plant spreads and sends down its root, going deeper and deeper, the root ministering to the gradually rising stem. But when it has grown to be a great tree, and spreads its broad, green leaves to the air, and is covered with its magnificent vases full of perfume, the topmost bloom will never forget for one single instant that humble root which, plunged down out of sight, is giving all its nourishment. Cut the connection between the top and the root, the top perishes, and the root likewise. The world is as a great tree in which the leaves that wave nearest to the heavens and drink in the sunshine, are after all the servants of the lowest roots that penetrate the earth. The hidden and the revealed are one; the power that the sun gives to the leaves goes down through the descending sap, and ministers to the utmost part of the roots, just as the roots, spread out, bring up also their offerings to minister to the top. So it is to be among men. We are but just learning it. The struggles go on in society, in its organizations of government, in its industries, all working in the same direction, all working toward the common welfare of men; impeded, checked, thrown back, but reasserting themselves, because they are the fruit and result of a Divine attraction which is universal, and which runs on through the ages in all time to the final consummation.

There be those here that walk in humble ways, for whom God's great triumph is prepared. When the iron door from life opens, and the golden hinges of the gate of the heavenly city are turned, there shall go forth to meet them those who have been blessed by them and sent on before — innumerable ranks and bands, many of them little children of glorified faces, that shall move without feet, and fly without wings; for such are not the adjuncts of spirit life. They shall come round about us who have by faith and patience achieved victory. We shall behold the great congregation of the noble gathered and garnered from all ages of the world, and from all nations. But we shall also behold Him who has redeemed our souls, and presided over all the days of our life; and Who, having loved us, loves us to the end.

What a consummation have we to-day! We stand on the ridge looking both ways to the past and the future. How many prayers are answered! How many tears, shed in darkness and silence, are made radiant now by the rising of the morning of joy. What lives have you abandoned! Upon what a glorious life you have entered! Some of you will be obscure. He on whose head God has placed His hand cannot be other than illustrious. Some of you will have much to bear. He that bears the cross of Christ can carry the world beside. You may die when you please and how you please. He dies into life who dies with Christ ministering to him. O, children of Christ, newly born! O, disciples of Christ, newly learning! I bid you Godspeed. If swept about by the trials of life — still recall this joyful hour. Stand steadfast and faithful. When we pass what has been called the river but is now the rill of death, scarcely wetting the soles of our feet, we shall stand with the ransomed of the Lord and lift up our heads crowned with eternal joy.

* *
*

When great structures are to rise, bands of workmen are deep down in the soil, digging; or with hammer and trowel working as the pile goes up, and at last is enclosed and completed. The men are paid and dismissed, but they will never forget as they go past it that they have worked on that building, although those who see the building will not know it. But when the temple of time shall have been completed, there is no man that ever carried shovel or hod, no man that ever worked at the foundation, or any part of the superstructure, that will be left out. Everybody that has sought righteousness and humanity and love will wear the decorations that Christ will give forth. In that millennium of love, in that grand judgment exposition of love—when you take the perspective of time, and look back, and see all cleared away, that long and weary course which to us now looks as tumultuous as a heap of stones, or as barren as a wilderness—we shall understand all. It will be the last grand interpreting sight as we look back and see the regular unfolding, stage by stage, long protracted because God is long-living, not measuring it by the term of human life, which is mis-measurement, but measuring it by the scale of Him that dwelleth in eternity and has time enough for the unfolding of thousands of years and ages. When we shall look back from that consummation, I think every doubt and strife and groan that we had on earth will be remembered only as children grown up remember the little troubles and trials of their early years.

* * *

I think there are hours when a man sees the solution of all the vexatious problems of life, being raised to a higher standpoint by a spiritual philosophy which is never enunciated in language, but is enunciated in experience. Sometimes it is only in the hour of death that the enunciation is made so that men look back upon their past life and business, and forward upon the life to come, and see what the things for which they have prayed, but which have been delayed or have been withheld wholly, have been working out in them and for them, by the sovereign grace of God.

* * *

If you believe in God, do not fret and worry. God is going to take care of the universe. I know there are multitudes of men who think they are sent into the world as God's vicegerents. They tell God in their prayers a good many things He never knew before, and He smiles at their advice in many other relations. But one thought ought to steady every man's heart. It is that God is perfectly wise and perfectly good, and is unfolding this earth individually and collectively in the ages. Let us accept God and rest in Him. Let us not worry nor fret ourselves at what men do, nor churches, nor nations, nor any other thing, but "trust in the Lord and do good".

Do the things you can, and do them cheerfully. Sing while you work. It is as cheap to trust as to fret.

⁎

If you do not know where the next loaf is to come from, what will you do? Going to be anxious, are you? What good will that do? Is Anxious a baker, that he will bring you bread?

⁎

Much of the anxiety of business is mere mosquito hunting. Everybody has his own mosquitos that fly by night or bite by day. There are few men of nerve firm enough to calmly let them bite. Most men insist upon flagellating themselves for the sake of not hitting their troubles.

⁎

The eagle sits upon the topmost crag, and the fowler far below draws vain arrows at him. There is not power in the bow to send the shaft so high as where he sits securely. And he who has made God his trust need fear neither bullet nor arrow, for no man can reach to touch him with harm there. In that hope ought we to live; we are the sons of God.

***

Fretting and anxious worrying not only do not promote prosperity, but they absolutely hinder it. What is the use of care and worry? Just so far as they are necessary to stimulate activity, they are beneficial; but the moment they go beyond that they are actual hindrances. I suppose that more than one-half of all the suffering of humanity is suffering on account of things that never happen. I think if you will look back and go over your life, and winnow it, when you take out all the fret and worry that really made you unhappy, and deprived you of bright, gleaming joy, you will find that it was the things which never happened that you worried about. I think you would find, on the other hand, that half of the good things that have really befallen you were things that you never dreamed of. It was the unexpected that came without your anxiety; and the things which you were fretting and worrying and twisting about incessantly, and which you allowed to take away your peace of mind, and oftentimes to take away your nerve, and unfit you for the battle of life, were things that did not come near you. You never learned from one day to another in that matter. You fretted on Monday just as you did on Sunday, and on Tuesday just as you did on Monday, and on Wednesday just as you did on Tuesday, and so on, year after year. You never learn anything about that. A man who attempted to mend a kettle would learn in an hour that every time he put a hot iron to it he made a bigger hole than he mended, and after a few trials he would give that up. But men go on making the same mistakes in the whole conduct and economy of their life-work.

It is a bad thing for a man to think too much about himself, to talk too much about himself, or to examine himself too much. The less he indulges in these things the better off he is. Let a man have a sense of duty, and take a right direction in life, and then sweep and lunge toward things outward as much as possible.

Do not make your sins like an Egyptian mummy, with its dried bones and muscles wrapped up in gummed hideousness. Let your past sins be buried, and if you want to go to the graveyard once in a while to see where you have laid them, go, but don't bring anything home with you.

There are many persons who live largely in rehashing their sins and their sense of guilt.

When a man has repented of his sins, that is enough. Kick them out; do not keep them like so many mummies or corpses in the house.

When you have done wrong and found it out, and

have changed to right, and have rectified all the ways in which your wrong doing has affected anybody else, that is the end; the sum is complete; you have no business to come back and sit down on your old grave-stones.

* * *

Paul said, "I count myself not to have apprehended; but this one thing I do, forgetting those things which are behind, and reaching forth unto those things which are before, I press toward the mark for the prize of the high calling of God in Christ Jesus." Paul persecuted; did he ever sit down and mourn over it? He spoke of it with tender self-reproach; but he had too much to do with the future to be groaning over the past; too much to do with the rebuilding to be criticising the old structure and delaying himself. "I have not become perfect, I have not reached my ideal, but I forget all the past," that is to say, "I do not stop to talk about my guilt, my wickedness, my unbelief, and all that sort of thing; I just let that go; it is past; but for the future my life lies there; I see what I mean to be, and I press toward it." Paul's life was in the future; he lived by hope as well as by faith and love.

* * *

Remorse is the disease of repentance; repentance is not remorse, and cannot be; and no remorse is healthy that lasts long and becomes chronic.

* * *

A great mother is one of God's windlasses around which is twined a silver thread; the child may go out and out; but, first or last, there will be a returning, and there will be a winding up, and he will come back again.

* * *

The unwritten poetry of a mother's heart would give to the world a literature beyond all printed words.

* * *

There is in every royal nature a holy of holies; a shrine within the shrine; a place of silence; the very place of germs, where thought, emotion, and being itself, begin. Into that comes not the most intimate. If any one has seen it, if any foot has trod it, we have banished ourselves and cannot return. There we meet God. There we meet ourselves. There we hide from love itself. But there a mother may come! And the soul is yet its own, though mother and God have looked upon its secret.

There is no miracle in conversion. It puts a man at school.

* * *

Some have an idea that a man may be a wicked

man up to a precise moment, and then, when the clock strikes twelve, a flash comes out, and he is converted, and he is all made over—no, no, no, no! I may say with perfect confidence that when the birds come from the South in early April, summer is coming—the precursors are here; the air is balmy; now then for the garden; now then for the farm; now then, go to work, husbandman; gardener, go to work. But the summer has not come. But the grass is springing, the flowers are peeping out—yes, bright heralds of the coming day. Seeds are coming up; truly all is right. But no man ever saw in the middle of March, rounded out and leaping forth, a whole summer with its grandeur and all its fruits. They come little by little. Religion may but have a beginning at any hour or under any condition. It is by a beginning; it is the start; for a true religion is one beginning as a grain of mustard-seed, the smallest of all seeds, yet grows and spreads itself. And to the dying day the man is not yet truly and perfectly religious; there is more to come out—so much more that the world is not fit for him any longer, and God takes him into a higher climate and into a nobler garden. It is putting on the harness, then; it is, in other words, developing in each man an educated and new life; subduing the primary tendencies of human nature and obliging them to conform to higher and nobler purposes.

* * *

The moment a man really wants to be a Christian,

he is one. The moment a man really wants to love me, he does love me. To be sure, where it is a thing that requires time and space and functional ceremony, the wishing for it is not having it; but where it is a thing that turns on the nature of the mind itself, wishing is having. The moment a man really wants to have knowledge, that moment he begins to have it. The want is the first step of knowledge.

God can convert a man in any way He pleases; and who are you, O theologian, that says He must convert him in just that way? I think that God converts a man that is slow and stolid, and has no imagination, in a way that is suited to that fact of human construction, and that He converts a man that is a poet in a way that is exactly adapted to that peculiar material He has got to work on. God does not convert paving-stones into roses, but He does convert roses from roots into bushes, and branches into roses. He works on men as He works on Nature. There are certain laws by which He works in Nature. Cause and effect are constant everywhere, and He works upon that greater Nature, the top of Nature, the sum and substance of Nature, human life and human experience, not in its basic forms, but experimental forms, according to His own will — that is to say, He adapts Himself to the facts that are in the man, brings him out along the way of experience that the man needs himself. And we take no glory from God.

When you come to the gate of heaven, you may be sure, if you knock and say, "Lord, Lord, open unto me", that you will not get in. A man that is fit to go in, always goes up without dreaming that God will not let him in. He expects to find the gate open.

There are a great many people that have had what is called a hope and lost it, or what is worse, kept it and dried it.

Conversion is to a man's soul just what ripening is to grapes. They hang in the right form; every one of them has skin and seeds, but all are sour. But just let them hang there long enough in the bright sunshine till it makes them sweet, and they are converted. That is exactly what conversion means to man. He hangs there, but sour, until he sees what is the power of God — the love of God and the spirit of God becomes sweetened to him.

Conversions are like the dawn of morning: they come and irradiate the very dewdrops and change them to jewels; they wake all birds, they wake all hearts and melodies. When a man has entered into the spiritual elements and knows what it means to be Christ's man, loving God and loving everybody, he begins to feel and wonder if there is anything on God's earth that is so ecstatic as love. If it is beautiful to love a single one by elective affinity, if the love by sympathy includes all men, is it lessened? It is glorified.

* * *

I tell you what, if it-s the Lord that converts men, I guess they'll know it, and other folks will be apt to know it too! Men are naturally like bags full of weed-seeds. The Lord first shakes 'em empty, and then fills 'em up with precious wheat. Now it stands to reason that if the Lord is shakin' a man inside out he'll know it.

* * *

Conversion is like the kindling in a soul of the light of love. No man is illuminated at conversion entirely; it is the rising light that shines brighter and brighter unto the perfect day. Before every part of the vast chamber of the human soul shall receive its light, time and suffering and experience must be passed through; but the beginning of the life of love — that, and only that, is conversion.

* * *

Any body that wants to keep Sunday to the Lord, will keep an eye to it all the week. My opinion is, that the reason why folks don't like Sunday is, that they don't know what it is to have a day full of real peace, up to the brim, from morning to night, and sweet as milk.

There are insects that fly at night, phosphorescing light when they have a mind to, flashing and shutting up, like Christians that flash on Sunday, and shut up all the week, flying through the dust of business!

Sunday is the common people's Magna Charta.

Sunday has been a generic and multiplex force, inspiring and directing all others. It is, indeed, the Sun's day.

Almost every cause which has worked benignly among us has received its inspiration and impulse largely from this One Solitary Day of the week.

Folks use their children as if they were garret pegs, to hang old clothes on—first a jacket, then a coat, and then another jacket. You have to take them all down to find either one. Our children go trudging all their lives with their load of names, as if they were old Jews returning with an assortment of clothes. People use their children as registers to preserve the names of aunts and uncles, parents and grandparents, and so inscribe them with the names of the dead, as if tombstones were not enough.

We smile at names. We weigh them in the scale of the ear for sweetness or smoothness. We call some, we reject others. We laugh at men's odd and awkward names, and quite justly too, it may be; since capricious whims, and vagrant fancies, or mere carelessness, so often select them. But sometimes a name is a history. It is like a pictured vase. We see the figures without thinking in what furnace those colors were fastened, and by what fire the glazing was fused. Is there in any history a record of the heart more touching and simple than that of old? "And it came to pass as Rachel's soul was departing, for she died, that she called his name Benoni"—Son of my Sorrow.

No grace that you have to tug and pull at is a grace that you yet possess. If a man wants to be humble, and thinks about being humble, and tries to be humble, and says, "What shall I do to make myself humble?" that is better than nothing, but he is on the lowest form in the school. He is an abecedarian. When a man has learned to be humble, he is humble spontaneously, and before he knows it. If a man is really meek, his meekness must not be on purpose. A man's meekness must leap out at once. He must have had such practice that it will come without any volition on his part. And so of generosity; so of forgiveness; so of that deep, unfolding love which shall spring up from generous impulses, and from forbearance, and from goodness, or from the nature of God, which overflows heaven, and deluges the universe itself. The feeling must be in you so strong, so full, so continuous, that it takes care of itself, and gushes out perpetually in every d.rection. And you are in this secret, higher religious state, just in proportion as you are involuntarily good, in distinction from being purposely and voluntarily good.

As long as a man thinks what he is going to say, he cannot be a public speaker. His speaking must get ahead of him, and he must go on behind it, and find out what he has said, as it were. That is the sensation he has. A man that is a poet is to be caught by inspiration, and carried on. And no man is more surprised than the man that has done these things to think that he has done them. A man that is working in the higher range is like a speaking trumpet, that never speaks but is spoken through. That is the feeling. The artist that stops and looks at his pallet, and says, "What shall I put there?—I do not know," has mistaken his vocation. A true artist puts the right thing there, and then says, "I wonder why I did it"? He is first led to do it, and then he analyzes and finds out the reason.

It is no compliment to Divine grace for a man who has been forty years in the church to get up and say, "I feel as though I was a vile and filthy rag." He is a vile and filthy rag to say that.

If God has been dwelling with a man for years, it is not for him to get up and speak of himself as having never had such a royal schoolmaster in his bosom.

Every man that begins to be a Christian, begins at the alphabetic forms. Day by day he grows in grace, and in the knowledge of the Lord and Saviour, Jesus Christ; but the grace must needs come first. It is action and reaction. All grace interprets Christ, and all knowledge of Christ acts back again to develop grace in the souls of men. Every Christian is in a process of sanctification, and his perfection comes hereafter and in heaven. The phenomenon of sanctification, the gradual progress of sanctification, is the application of this great truth which interprets the very genius of the whole Scripture—namely, that men come to a higher and higher knowledge of God through their own experiences. Christ becomes manifest to them more and more through long trials. Men learning patience for themselves, come to admire the infinite long-suffering and patience of God. A self-denying love—compassion for inferiors and for the imperfect—develops a true conception of what is that wonderful love of God in Christ Jesus that saves a world of sinners. By laying down our lives, or by holding them not for our own benefit, but for those that need us, we have learned what is the power of the Lord Jesus Christ, and what is the meaning of His covenant of grace, and of His example, and of His atonement, and of the elementary form of all that constitutes what may be called the scheme of redemption. They are all of them evolved in the human kind from the incipient experiences of God's people.

There is nothing so beautiful as Christlikeness carried out into life by Christian men. There is nothing that so penetrates. It is the best cosmetic for homely folks. You cannot change their features or anything of that kind, but you can change their expression. The artist stands before the canvass and paints on this side of it; but the true holiness goes on the other side, and strikes through the colors of the face, and out comes the beauty of expression, the noblest, divinest beauty there is in this world.

When it is time for you to die, God will give you dying grace. It is for you to find out how to live with living grace, and not all the time to live as if you were just going to die.

Although there is great blessing in a prayer-meeting, no prayer-meeting on earth is such a means of grace as a man's own store.

* * *

Use fiction as you would spices in your diet. No man takes a quart of cloves, nor exhausts the cruet at a single meal. These things are to be used with moderation to season one's food with, but they are not to be used alone; and so fictions, while they are not to be assorted too exclusively, may be used with discretion to season life with.

* * *

A reading of fiction which throws off care, or a reading of fiction which brings knowledge to men's minds — as does much of the fiction that is written nowadays — such a reading of fiction is beneficial. He who reads fiction to rest himself, to refresh himself, to lift himself above the dead level of the vulgar real, reads it to his advantage and profit; but he who reads it to abide in it, never giving back a better man to his every-day household or business' duties, is hurt by it. It has decomposed the texture of his mind. He is not so good a man as he was before. And a man to be benefited by the reading of fiction not only must be lifted up by it above the affairs of earth, but must come back to those affairs again with renewed strength. It is said that Antæus renewed his strength when he touched the ground; but we renew our strength when we rise into the air. We derive our strength from the invisible rather than from the visible.

* * *

A true Christian is like a well-plumbed house. He has but to turn on the light, and it is there always. He has but to turn on the faucet, and rivers and wells are at his service. An untrained man is like a family in the lower countries, where he has to go to the distant spring to bring in every bucket of water that he uses for culinary purposes; and what we want is not to have to pump up right feeling, at the right time, but to have the right feeling, as it were, in the very structure of the soul, so that we have it always when needed. A man who has no patience but that which comes from instant reflection will have very little; but a man who has trained his patience so that it acts through habit automatically will, perhaps, not have the reputation of being patient; but if not, it is because the work is so perfect. It is the art of art to conceal art.

* * *

Every Christian may and should so live as to have all his views of life clear and settled as to right and wrong; so as to recognize and obey moral truths as readily as the senses do physical truths. All our physical life is formed of habits, we are accustomed to perfect spontaneity of affections; is it then mysticism to say that we may live in the higher range of faculties on the same point as we do in the lower spontaneously. When the soul is touched by the spirit of God, bathed and suffused in the spirit of love, the mind harmonized in every part, love casting out not fear only, but all impurity, weakness, impediment—this is the highest state of Christian living.

No two persons on God's earth have the same thing to do in order to be a Christian.

Where two persons are identical in their religious life, I conclude that one or the other of them is mistaken; for every man has his individual character; and religion consists in the development of each man according as God, in his providence, made him, and where a man is developed so he will not be just like anybody else.

Much evil comes from the habit which persons have of comparing themselves with one another. Suppose a revival should break out in a band of music, and the different instruments should undertake to determine whether they were right or not by seeing whether they were like each other or not. The haut-boy is in great distress of mind because it does not sound like the bassoon. "If the bassoon is right, then I am wrong," it says. The flute is discouraged because it is not like the violoncello; and it says, "If that is right, I ought not to be here". The violin is very much concerned because it is not like the French horn. So each instrument is discontented because by comparison, it has found that it differs from the others. But is not each a musical instrument in its own way? Is it not the business of each to be musical according to its peculiar nature? They have all to be brought to some concert-pitch, so that their sound shall combine and harmonize; but an orchestra is made up of all sorts of instruments, some wooden, some stringed, and some brass; and each of them has its own temperament, or tone; and when chorded and played according to their kind, they unite in making harmonious music; and the richness of this music depends upon the variety of instruments which are working in a certain line, in a given direction, and in harmony with each other. It is variety which makes the power and beauty of every orchestra.

* * *

The exaltations of men lie not in their outward conditions, not in the praises of men, but in the qualities of their own nature, in the lines of light and knowledge by which they live; and he that becomes a Christian and lives in the heroic mood of Christianity stands highest, is best prepared to meet the buffetings of misfortune, can live in cheer and patience and hope.

* * *

There is no apology needed for the rose — it is its

own apology; the grapes in a vineyard make themselves manifest to every passer-by; and every man to be a Christian after Christ's method should so live that when persons look upon him they shall say, "It is lovely! It is beautiful!" All acerbity, all over-rigidity, all timidity that circumscribes rational labor, all unnatural self-denials, everything that makes a man appear to the simple-minded other than genial and loving, is a contradiction of Christianity. You are bound so to carry your religion that when men shall see your light shining they shall want to be Christians too, and glorify your Father which is in heaven.

Christians are like folks that have brushes and a palette, but not much paint. When they undertake to establish good and overcome evil, the qualities, the pigments, are wanting. A languid, low-toned color of goodness never overcomes anything. It must be positive, full of blood, radiant as an angel. Then a man shall go out with a conception of goodness into the community, and wherever he goes he will carry conviction to evil, so far as conviction can be produced at all.

The fruit of the Spirit is that which is underlaid by culture, but culture itself is not it. The text is not the precious thing, it is the meaning in the text that is precious. A farm must have its implements, but it is the harvest that is of value, and they are relative. If a man can make a good crop with the poorest implements he is better off than his neighbor who has ten times better instruments but a poorer crop. And if a man can make out of heresies a better Christian life than another man does out of his orthodoxy, he is nearer to God than the orthodox man.

It is the poverty of Christian experience that makes infidelity; it is the bad lives of Christians that make men doubt whether there are any real lives of Christians.

I believe in the apostolicity of the churches, I believe in the descent from the Apostles, I believe that that man that is the most humble, the most self-sacrificing, the lovliest man before God and with the deepest love, he is apostolic. There is no descent from the Apostles except in the apostolic life.

Do not think because you cannot compare with some other one that you are not a Christian. God never called you to be any one else than yourself. Persevere, be equal to the occasion God sends.

* * *

True Christian living is true Christian teaching. Living faith among us is the remedy for infidelity outside of us.

* * *

The Christian is like a ground diamond, that has no light in itself, but flashes back from every facet the light the sun gives it.

* * *

What is the difference between a just man and a good man? A just man may stand like an icicle; he may repel rather than attract; he is fixed in one or two elements; there is no recurring impulse in his justice; it does not swell and contract like the tides; it does not go out and come roaring back; it lacks variety; it has almost the constancy of fate in it. But a good man, a good-natured man, is a man whose mind is all the time bubbling over with strong impulses, and impulses along the line of fixed habits. For such a man there is sympathy, love, co-operation, and rejoicing.

* * *

A man who is a true Christian ought to be the most trusted by the folks that know him best. His servants ought to believe in him. The companions of his leisure ought to believe in him. The folks that see him on a journey away from home for months ought to believe in him. The horse that has not a record is of no account. He may have it in him, but he is of no account. It is not until you put him on his speed and time him by the watch, that you can tell whether he is good for anything or not. It is when men are timed that they break down. It is the man who, on the journey and in the distant capital, as well as at home, on all the days of the week as well as on Sunday, has an established luminous Christian character, and abides by it — it is that man who goes forth as a real teacher of the gospel of Christ.

The conditions of life are such that, first or last, every right living person, every person striving to live by a higher standard than that of the community around him — those who are seeking to live only by this standard, will be brought into a necessity of patience, and a patience of faith and not of sight. There are a large number of men who come into life with an unbalanced interior, with a disproportionate allocation of faculties. There are some who have mighty passions and a slender reason. There are some who have a very strong temper and but little restraining power. The inharmoniousness of men's interior is such as to be a separate study of itself. Men are like an instrument which is at discord with its own self, and cannot send forth symphonic music with any success. So there are many persons whose business, whose problem, whose battle in life consists in some sort of readjustment by education of the disproportionate elements which go to constitute their nature.

There is no misfortune in the world like having one's ideal lowered. Our ideal of character is the rudder by which we steer.

I think that a man ought so to live by a standard of honor, truth, and manliness, that he can afford to sleep with himself without any fear or trouble. I wonder that some men can ever keep company with themselves. It is bad company.

* * *

The destruction of ideal standards is utterly ruinous to our manhood.

There is that prophetic gift in every soul of any elevation by which there hangs over every step a vision of something higher, and better, and nobler, and sweeter, and purer. Every man who is really and fully organized on a noble pattern, has hovering over him a vision of angels transcendently more beautiful than any embodiment of it. He has conceptions of truth infinitely more grand than any exhibitions of truth which he sees on earth. Beauty flames in the heavens with color brighter than any that can be reproduced in this world. How do they who attempt to fulfill the offices of friendship, find every day that they sit in judgment upon themselves because they have not half way come up to their conception of its patience, of its disinterestedness, of its gentleness, of its faithfulness.

The musician is charmed with the song that in his imagination he seems to hear angels sing; but when he attempts to write it down with his hands he curses the blundering rudeness of material things, by which he cannot incarnate so spiritual a thing as his thought. It is all torn; it is stripped of its plumage, as it were, and reduced to captivity. The true orator is a man whose unbroken speech is a thousand times better than his utterance. The true artist is not a man who can look upon the thing he has colored and say, "It transcends what I saw"; but a man who says, "Oh! if you could see what I saw when I first tried to make this, you would think this most homely".

This excelsior of every soul; this sense of something finer, and nobler, and truer, and better — so long as this lasts there is in every man a nascent inspiration which tends to look away from self — which certainly does not incline a man to measure himself by his fellowmen. It is vulgar for a man to be satisfied with himself because he is better than his fellowmen. Every man should have something outside of himself, and outside of his fellowmen by which to measure himself. Every single day should be a day to you of royal discontent.

You never thought as well as you ought to think.

You never meant as highly as you ought to mean. You never planned as nobly as you ought to plan. You never executed as well as you ought to execute. Over the production of the scholar, over the canvas of the artist, over the task of the landscape gardener, over the pruner's knife, there ought to hover, perpetually, his blessed ideal, telling him, "Your work is poor — it should be better"; so that every day he should lift himself higher and higher, with an everlasting pursuit of hope which shall only end in perfection when he reaches the land beyond.

If all other men were but four feet high, a man five feet would be considered a giant. If you put your standard low enough, a man can always judge favorably about himself.

Live to-day by your standard, and so far as you come short, say, "I am sorry; but, Lord, I come to Thee" — and take a new start.

Men without faults are apt to be men without force. A round diamond has no brilliancy. The faults of great, generous natures are often over-ripe goodness or the shadow which their virtues cast.

* * *

Men are not willing to admit that they are assailable and vincible in the point where they are weakest. Yet every man must guard the point of weakness in himself. And watchfulness must not be general, or vague, or theoretical. Neither must it be the same as this man's or that man's, whose weakness is different from yours. Your watch must be set over against that which is weak in you. Each man's watchfulness should be according to his temperament and constitution.

* * *

Every man should know what are the circumstances, the times, and the reasons in which he is liable to sin. There are a great many who neglect to watch until the proper time and seasons for watching have passed away. There are many men who are like a ship aground. When the tide is out she does not leak— of course not; but as soon as the tide comes up and surrounds her, she leaks at every seam, and is filled with water. And so there are men who, when the tide is up, are perfectly whelmed, but who, when the tide goes out, are perfectly free.

* * *

Faults are often stepping stones to heinous sins.

* * *

Faults unmatched tend to run together, and so become far more potent than they are in detail.

What on earth is so small as mist-drops? And even when chilled by the cold in the atmosphere, a few of them come together, they fall as scattered drops of rain upon the ground. They can hardly make a leaf wink. And yet, when these drops fall in rapid succession, and continuously, and drop finds drop, and they run along together, a rill is found. And another rill meets that one. And by and by there is a stream as big as your wrist. And such streams are the fathers of rivers, mighty and irresistible. And little things, that do not amount to much in themselves, if there are enough of them and they flow together long enough, constitute irresistible forces.

* * *

There is nothing more easily crushed than a small spider; but if you let him alone he breeds other spiders; and they will breed still other spiders. Did you ever see what a swarm of spiders will spring from one egg? And yet, all of them, soon after they are hatched, not only are predatory, but are weavers. Great is the tribe of weavers. Each goes to work to make himself a house—and that is well enough for a spider, that does not know any better. One of these spiders, perhaps, is in my window, and sets about making his house there. He does not seem to amount to much; but he has power that is not to be despised. If I were to say that that speck of a spider was an antagonist of the sun, and that it would beat the sun all hollow, you would laugh me to scorn; but it is so. For presently he has a brood of spiders — five hundred of them — and they set to work to spin their webs, and run them from side to side, from top to bottom, and from corner to corner; and by and by the window is covered all over. And particles of dust, flying through the air, settle on it, and fill up the little spaces between the threads. And after a while the spiders spin other webs and cover over the first ones. And the dust settles on these. And in a year, let the sun get through that window if he can! Big as he is, and strong as he is, the spider is more than a match for him.

So a multitude of little faults obscure moral sight, and dim a man's outlook, and substantially put out his eyes, so that he cannot see. Although each one of them is very small they are very effective. Beware of faults that tend to reproduce themselves continually.

If anger is up, good nature is down. If you want to get anger down, don't try to push it down — that won't do, but go to the other end and pry up good nature.

Books are the windows through which the soul looks out.

Books are grindstones and whetstones for a man's mind.

Those are true books which, like glasses, serve to enlarge that which lies outside and beyond themselves.

The slowest thing that can be done in this world is the building up of moral character. Many persons think that there is a lightning-like process by which men's characters can be built up by the Holy Ghost. They think that when God by His Spirit strikes the soul He knocks the old nature out of it; and that then the man rises up a new creature in Christ Jesus. If you regard this as a mere figure, there is some truth in it; but if you literalize it, and test it scientifically, and say that God changes man's nature in an instant as by a flash of lightning it is not true. It is as far from the analogy of nature as it can possibly be. For there is no work that is so important, and none that is so high, as the creation of manhood in Christ Jesus; and there is no work that takes so much time; there is no work that is so slow; and there is no work in which men are tempted to be so impatient.

The work of soul-unfolding is slow because it is so

voluminous; it is slow because it belongs to so high a sphere; it is slow because it requires the operation of both human and Divine influences. It is a work which cannot be concentrated.

* * *

Men who want harvests must work and wait for them. Men recognize this in material things, but they think it is different in spiritual things. They say, "It holds good in the realm of matter, but not in the moral kingdom of God". My friends, God's moral kingdom is the same as His natural kingdom. There is no distinction between these two kingdoms except that which you make by words. They are parts of a grand unit. They are one and the same thing. Nature begins in inorganic matter, and rises through sentient being to the throne of God itself. It is one stupendous whole. The same analogical laws run through it from top to bottom. The same great Divine processes and methods belong to every part of it. And that God, who will not make the wilderness to bud and blossom as the rose without industry, will not cause flowers and fruits to spring up in the arid soul of a man without industry. If, therefore, you are attempting to bring up your children by prayer, I tell you, you are like a man who goes out to hunt, and says, "The great power of hunting lies in the bow", and does not carry any arrows with him, and twangs at a deer, but does not hurt him; or you are like a man who goes out, and says, "The power of hunting lies in the arrow", but does not carry any bow; so that when he pulls the arrow over his hand down it goes at his feet and does not kill anything. For successful hunting there must be a good bow, and a good arrow, and a good man behind them both. If these conditions are complied with, you will hit, if there be any hit in you. Says the Divine Word, "Work out your own salvation with fear and trembling"—there is the arrow; "for it is God that worketh in you"—there is the bow. The two things are necessary.

* * *

A man's character is his reality. It is the acting, moving force of his being. Reputation is the impression which he has made upon other men—it is their thought of him. Our character is always ourselves, but our reputation is in others.

* * *

Men seem to think that the imagination is one of the lighter faculties; that it may be used sportively in alliance with sensuous beauty; but the imagination is to be used in connection with the reason as well as the senses; and these elements combined give higher ideals than can be attained by the senses alone. The whole race goes from the lower to the higher planes of life through the imagination.

***

No man without imagination can by any possibility be an acute observer, nor a sound reasoner even upon physical facts, still less upon truths that involve some mental qualities.

***

Words mean whatever they have the power to make us think of when we look on them. Flowers mean what sentiment they have the power to produce in us. The image which a flower casts upon a sensitive plate is simply its own self-form; but, cast upon a more sensitive human soul, it leaves there not mere form, but feeling, excitement, suggestion. God gave it power to do that, or it would not have done it.

***

Imagination is the very marrow of faith.

***

Lord's Supper belongs to every one who desires to lead a Christian life, and puts his hope and trust in the Lord Jesus Christ, whether he belongs to another communion, or whether he belongs to none. If in your inmost soul you desire to live Christ-like, and wish to avow the Lord as your Saviour, and to follow him faithfully, and this is offered to you, you have a right to take it.

***

To-day we are called on for a renewed expression of fealty and fidelity. The taking of this bread and the drinking of this wine is emptiness itself, unless we can quicken our faith and our thought by some such identification with Christ as shall give meaning to these materials. Are you broken as a loaf is broken. Is your heart wrung as the cluster of grapes is wrung out into wine? Is the very blood, almost, of suffering wrung out of you? Christ the Sufferer, Christ the Burden-Bearer, Christ—though he first crowned himself least and lowest—is your Master; and are you willing to follow Him in the way of suffering, in the way of strife, and make proof of what love is, not by the joyousness of an inflamed love, but by the power of love to bear, to endure, to suffer? How much that love is, is not to be told on the strings of the lute! How much that love is, is not to be told on the gales of perfumed summer! How much that love is, can never be made known by the sweetest descantings of poetry and oratory! How much that love is, tears and wounded hands and lacerated hearts tell! Suffering is the test of love. Are you, to-day, willing to be a disciple of the suffering and self-sacrificing Saviour, and to go forth out of the camp to meet and rejoice with Him in His disfigurement and in all His sacrifice, and so reign with Him in heaven; and, when He shall come with all His father's angels, to be glorified in the final victory of the universe?

I cannot bring back my little child, but I can take a locket and look at his face; and he springs to life in my inward thought. There are scenes in my childhood that I cannot tread again, but a very simple memorial, a little dried flower, or some little yellow faded note, bring back again with a resurrection of the memory the sweet sense of an early experience. There are sorrows that come again as if they had never departed, and so by some such very simple symbol we can bring again before us the Saviour broken for us, his blood shed for us; and bring into our mind the royalty of love suffering for those that it loves, and dying to give them life; weakened, dishonored, slain, that we might be strengthened, glorified, and everlastingly saved.

If you feel your need of God, and have faith that He feels a need of you; if your heart has a throb of answering gratitude for the great goodness with which He has been kind to you, you have the conditions that justify you in partaking of this Lord's Supper.

Church membership is not the ground for the Lord's Supper. The ground is spiritual need.

* * *

Let the affairs of life call you up step by step. Do not force your way. Do not commit burglary on success.

* * *

If a man will have a golden fish, let him go to the side of the stream of life calmly, put in his hook discreetly, and lift out his prey with an easy and even pull. But if he threshes back with full swing, ten to one he will dash his luck to pieces.

* * *

Take the lowest seat, and work your way up. Let a man be called up always. Do your work wherever you are, and do it faithfully and so contentedly that men will want you one step higher and will call you up. And when you get there, do your work so thoroughly well and so contentedly that they will want you still higher. The more you do your work well the more they will want you still higher, and higher, and higher. Be drawn up. Do not force yourself up. That leads to chicanery, to pretence, to mistakes, and even to temptations and crimes.

* * *

There is not one man that is smart where there are twenty men that think they are; and many men are smart only as flies are; they make a world of buzzing, but do not make much else.

It is not what a man finds that does him good but what he does.

First get your fish to bite, then see that you so land them that they are good for something.

You cannot succeed in life by spasmodic jerks. You cannot win confidence nor earn friendship, nor gain influence, nor attain skill, nor reach position by violent snatches. One sort of men lose by too much caution, another kind by too much largeness. One waits too long, another does not wait long enough.

God will not thank you for the parings, the peelings, the chaff, the shucks, of your time. If there is an hour when your thoughts are clearer and your affections are stronger than at any other time, take that hour for God. Serve God with your best faculties. Serve Him not only with the best times and seasons but with the best feelings that you have. We are to take care that we keep our most royal hours and our most golden moods for His service.

A man that can put into exact words what he feels, does not feel much.

There is a wisdom of feeling, as well as of thought. Calculation is as often wrong as inspiration. The intuitions of our moral sentiments seldom mislead us. The passions need the rein and curb, but moral sentiments need the spur.

Come — that is the thing — with a deep experience, if you have it; without a deep experience, if you have it not; .with a great tumult, if you cannot help it; without much tumult if it please God that it should be so. It is come back to God at any rate.

Our finer feelings are like the evening primrose, all the sunlight but shuts them closer. And yet, when evening comes and dews are falling, if you will watch, you shall see the twilight with gentle influence unroll them one by one, with visible motion, each blossom throwing forth, as it opens, its offering of delicate color.

The finest essences of human life are those that elude all philosophy and all language. Tell me, is there anything more exquisite than a mother's love for her babe? And though she were a poet, lyrical like Sappho, though she were like Browning, though she were like the rarest spirits that ever lived, what mother does not know, when she would put that which is the very exquisite royalty of emotion into lauguage, that no language was ever made that expressed it. Language can point the way to where the feeling is, and give some general conception of it; but the beauty, the glory, the voice of the feeling escapes.

The only use of feeling in repentance is to make a man change. That which will make a man change is feeling enough, and the old midnight of horror that does not change a man is not good for anything. Men say it is being sorry for your sins. Yes; that is an element of it; that is a primary element of it. But what is the use of being sorry for your sins if you do not quit them? No use at all. Sorrow is not broth that gives any digestible quality to a man's sin. The only use of feeling bad at all is to remedy something. If you feel bad in bone or muscle or nerve, on account of dissipation, the feeling bad about it, over and above the physical ache, is simply reforming your manners, your way of living; that is all it is good for. Pain is the incitement to reformation.

Feelings are like drops of water. They form rivers

and roll slowly on, with only here and there a sounding fall, and empty themselves into the eternities.

You do not need to wait for any systematic belief, or for any special change. Take the duty that stands next to you, and attempt to do it for God's sake, and continue doing it, and the proper discharge of your obligations will of itself develop in you a spiritual state. The tendency of right-doing is to raise the doer into a higher mood.

If right feelings do not produce right conduct they die out; and if right conduct does not produce right feelings it is because you do not let it. Every good deed that a man does is like the germ of a plant. Give it a chance to grow, and the earth beneath it will counsel it to shoot up; and up it will come. Every right thing done, if it be not hindered, will be fruitful in spiritualizing the mind; and a spiritualized mind will occupy itself in doing right things.

As promised pleasures bear no proportion in realization to anticipation, so the exigencies we esteem most dangerous and painful, bring with them remunerations nowhere else to be found. Sometimes when it has seemed as if telling the truth were like laying down life, we find ourselves suddenly superior to whatever man may do or say or think. The loose and floating joys which men call pleasure, are not to be compared with the triumph of rising above difficulties, when we break through the crust of flesh, and sound the depths of our immortality; this is a transcendent, a rarer joy than aught else can bestow. The reason of this is in the philosophy of it. Christian self-denial is the triumph of a higher feeling over a lower one. When the lower powers and passions are completely subjugated, and habitually under the control of conscience and love, the conscious self-denial ceases. Every Christian should doubt himself if self-denial is as hard after ten years as at the beginning. Where there is but little drill and training there will be hard fighting, but we should deny ourselves until the feeling of self-denial ceases.

**
* *

Self-denial is that by which we put down the inferior things for the sake of the ascendency of superior things. It runs in music, it runs in the painter's art, it runs in sculpture and in architecture, it runs in husbandry and in statesmanship, it runs everywhere. There is not in the world any way by which a man comes to himself in the higher realms, except by steps of self-denial; and when Christ says, with larger scope and more profound spiritual meaning, "If any man would come after Me, let him deny himself, and take up his cross and follow Me", it is a truth as wide as the sphere; but how different in the understanding of men from what it was in the pronunciation of our Master!

A man that is so shallow as to live merely for himself very soon exhausts himself.

We do not go far enough in our self-denials; we go just so far as to make them taste bitter, and not to make them taste good with the heroism and the triumphs on the other side.

Is gratifying one's self the end of life? Is that the Christian love? Has any man a right to hold himself in his class, and have no intercouse with those who are beneath him except that of a patron, and a far-off patron, sending down kindnesses to them? Is there a man that is superior that does not owe himself to those who are inferior? There is no other gift that is so worthy of giving as one's self. God, when He would show his love to the world, gave himself; and what are you, that you shall not give yourselves? The higher you are, the more you owe yourselves to the lowest and least; and you owe, not what you take in your hand, but what you have in your heart. You owe your taste, your sensibility, your accomplishments, your knowledge, your inner man. It is by the medicine of a living soul that dead souls are brought to life.

* * *

A man who does not know how to learn from his mistakes turns the best schoolmaster out of his life.

* * *

It is better for a man to make mistakes striving, than to make no mistakes supine, dead. Life is able to qualify mistakes.

* * *

Even mistakes are providences; for as the axe is made sharp by that which it loses on the grindstone, so men are made sharp by that which they lose through blunders that fit them for the next encounter.

* * *

Impulse springs up, and, like a spark, dies out; but purpose brings brand to brand, feeds the fire and keeps its luminosity and heat steadily going. It gives unity to action. It does not trust to moods at all, knowing that they come and go like tides. It even excites impulse, which first excited it; for all will grows out of emotions; and if guided by the intellect, interfused by those methods by which the impulses are gratified, not only once or twice, but continuously in the future, it is the main-spring of industry. It connects industry with industry. Will power is the purpose that sees the line of action between things, organizes it, and carries it on. Unless there were some such determining, connecting element, man's life would be like a bushel of marbles, simple impulses in juxlaposition, but not an organic unity.

This world is a great groaning machine which needs lubrication and God-sent humor to make its wheels run smooth.

It is a great thing to have a sense of humor. To go through life with no sense of the humorous and ridiculous, is like being in a wagon without springs.

I never saw any harm in laughing. If it's a sin I can't see what the Lord lets so many funny things happen for. I don't go and make things funny! They come to me. The whole world is full of queer things, and it isn't my fault if I see them.

The way to lift a soul up into the arms of God is to put another soul under it, and lift it up by its power. The true gospel is that of soul on soul in this world.

Men are not music boxes, which, when wound up, carry their own players inside of them; but they are harps, which must be touched from without. Each man's heart, therefore, must be touched by other men. We are to touch other men's hearts. Other men's hearts are belfries, and there we must ring out all our chimes.

Every man should learn to look upon his business as a calling that, while it brings to him support, and it may be affluence, and even distinction, in the main is a factor of benevolence, and is developing him by methods that very largely multiply the happiness, the convenience, and the welfare of his fellowmen.

The real secret and center of the universe is, "God is love"; and that love overmasters anarchy of force; and that the genius of Divine government in all time, as it shall be seen at the close of time, is care for the weak.

All those men who have the spirit of Christ are giving themselves forth a ransom for many, not in the same sense that He did, but according to the measure of their power and of their sphere. We are of Christ when we imitate him by giving ourselves for others.

Love the Lord thy God with all thy heart, and thy neighbor as thyself. And in the proportion in which you find in yourself that humanizing and Divine tendency, care for those that need care, the distribution of yourself, your treasures of knowledge, your refinements of beauty and of civilization, the power of your hand, the power of your treasure, the power of your heart—in proportion as these go out to men just in the ratio of their need, in that proportion you will reproduce Christ, in that proportion you will reproduce God in the imagination and in the heart of men.

* * *

The power of the State lies in the bottom of it. Take care of that and you take care of the whole.

* * *

If there is any orthodoxy in the world that is valid to the judgment-day, and beyond it, it is the orthodoxy of right loving. On these two — love to God and love to man — hang all the law and the prophets, said the Lord Himself. Love is the end of the law for righteousness; love doeth no injury to any one; love is the Gospel.

* * *

"Who is my neighbor?" Anybody that knows you is your neighbor. Everybody that I meet is my brother. God is a universal father, the human race is a universal family, man is brother to man, men are kindred the world over; and no man can really learn how to love until he comes into that disposition of the soul by which he has sympathy, longing, yearning, good-will, toward every human creature.

God's kingdom — that is, the ideal mankind, looked at in the light and under the influence of Jesus Christ — is not divided up by artificial lines, but is an absolute united brotherhood. From the spiritual plane, looking down upon the human race, it is one great family; and as God is the Father, the whole race is His household; and all the diverse scattered elements of the human family are, after all, interiorly grouped together in the eye of God and of His providence, as one great unity, one vast brotherhood.

This brotherhood of man does not mean absolute equality, nor desert absolutely alike. It is entirely consistent with the doctrine of inferiors and superiors — with the relative superiority which belongs to power, and the relative inferiority which belongs to want of power. Because some are high, and because they are relatively superior, it does not necessarily follow that they are separated from those who are inferior to them by reason of demerit or weakness or sin.

The glory of the household is the strength of the strong and the weakness of the weak. There is nothing in the household so strong as the weakness of the cradle. There is nothing in the household so reverend as the weakness of the venerable father or mother that sits trembling in the chair. To the one extreme or the other of weakness, all strength, all virtue, and all manliness bow. And in the human race there should be the enlisting of strength in behalf of weakness. The power of knowledge, of refinement, of culture, of the arts, etc., in a strong race, are so many overtures of generous bounty, so many means of beneficence, so many filaments of union, by which the weak are to be bound to the strong. The welfare of the whole is to be sought by the whole.

An absolute brotherhood is quite consistent with subordination, with relative position, the high being high without detriment to the low, or rather the high beings almoners of God's bounty to the low. The attempt to level all men to an absolute equality, whether of bodily, mental, moral, or political and secular conditions, is a madman's attempt.

If there should be rebellion in the fields, and the grass should be jealous of the forests, and should say to the pines, and hemlocks, and beeches, and birches, and maples, and oaks, and hickories, "Bring down those high heads of yours", it would not make the grass grow any higher. Grass is grass, and trees are trees; and no amount of railing on the part of the one will make it equal to the other. No destruction of the top is going to lift up the bottom. There is no way in which the bottom can go up except as the top goes up — by brain-power, in the right spot, at the top of the head and not at the bottom.

The brotherhood of man does not imply any notions of equality, either actual or possible. To the end of the world there will be gradations.

Emotion with intellect — emotion as the bow and the intellect as the arrow — that is preaching.

Many and many a river works. The Merrimac runs with a small channel. It is called a prodigious river; but I could almost ford it. Where are its waters? For a hundred miles they are busy turning vast wheels. They have turned out to the right and to the left, and gone to work; and that is better than for them to be in the middle of a deep channel, and not work. So there are great hearts that turn currents of emotion into actual practical deeds.

Many persons think emotion is religion; but it is not. A person may have such rapturous views of

God, of heaven and the rest that remaineth for the people of God, as to be unfitted for either heaven or earth. It is safe and wholesome to have intense feelings, high excitements, if they take on practical forms; but it is neither safe nor wholesome to have such feelings and excitements if they do not take on such forms.

* * *

The true test in religion is not how impressionable one is. I put an Æolian harp in my window. The evening breeze having nothing to do, and finding the harp in the window, courts it, and an interchange of sweet sounds goes on. I take a crow-bar and put that in the window. The same wind sweeps over it, but it does not sing. Why did the harp sing? For no reason except that its nature is impressionable. There was no merit in what it did. Why did not the crow-bar sing? Because it was made a crow-bar. Some men are like crow-bars and some like Æolian harps; but if a man is like an Æolian harp, it is no credit to him that he sounds quickly; and if a man is like a crow-bar it is not his fault that he does not sound readily.

* * *

There are some men who are prodigiously joyful in religion, but to whom no more merit is due than to the trumpet that sounds loudly when a strong man blows it. There are other persons who have slow, methodical, unexcitable natures; and, looking at these excitable people they say, "If I really were a good Christian man, there is what I should be; but I cannot get up to where they are. I wish I could, God be merciful to me a sinner." Now, these unemotive men are as true to their nature as are those emotive men, and very likely are better; for although emotive men are sensitive to feeling, the unemotive men never use their feeling as a cascade to fill the air full of flying drops and vapor; they use it rather as a mill-stream with which to turn the wheel of purpose and activity.

Suppose one could say, "It is a good thing to be a genius, but I am not one. I should be very glad to be a composer like Rossini, or Mozart, or Handel, or Haydn, or Beethoven, or Wagner; but I am not. I cannot make the air melodious; I cannot send marching through space grand processions of sounds that stir the imagination of men; but I have love and joy; and my joy rings out perpetually such music that if it is not heard on earth it must be heard on the other side. I have constant joy. Men cannot help feeling it. I sleep, and hear bells ringing. I wake, and they are ringing still. The chimes of God and of the eternal world are forever in my soul, which is the belfry of God." How many men glory in that? How many men are proud because they have love and joy?

If a man is born a crow, let him crow; but if he is born a nightingale, let him sing and not crow.

A true Christian man should be the freest, most joyous, upright, frank, most lovable.

* * *

There are joys that mock the senses, there are joys that lift up almost within sound of the harpings at heaven's gate.

* * *

Joy comes to us as the chestnut comes, the burr full of prickles, but in the interior, sweet and most toothsome nuts.

* * *

A man may have joy of one sort and of another and of another; but it is when the whole man is composed into a harmony in Jesus Christ that he hears those sounds of true joy that will not die away. We are like an orchestra in our life. Suppose that in an orchestra the instruments did not care for each other, every one of them striving to take the lead of all the rest; suppose the piccolo should undertake to squeal away in the altitudes and drown all the others; or suppose that the sharp piercing clarionet should feel itself to be the whole music that there was in the band; suppose the old wheezy bassoon should say, "No, I am here also"; and suppose the tenor and the bass were at conflict with each other, each seeking to make itself heard and be dominant; what would you think of that for music? It is where they are all attuned to each other in common concert pitch, where they all harmonize with each other, that we have true music. The broad ocean is a unit, and it constantly comes back again to unity.

So it is in character. A superficial joy, a joy of the senses, a mere joy that hath in it neither time nor eternity, but a flash — that is not the ideal of Christian joy that I would hold before you; it is that due submission of every part of your nature to harmony in yourself as the immediate inspiration of God.

A true Christian development in man, formed after the pattern of Jesus Christ, is full of joy of every kind from the lowest to the highest scale; and as in the harp the deepest note of every chord all the way up to the shrillest is musical, so in a truly Christian disposition we have the right of joyfulness in all things that are becoming manhood and womanhood.

Gentleness is not a quality of not having vim. When a man is strong and energetic, and at the same time uses his strength and energy and power with sweetness, that is gentleness. See the great swarthy smith as he returns from the anvil, every muscle herculean after the day's labor, washing himself that he may come back to his own complexion. As the little child totters out to him, see with what ineffable sweetness he gathers up the little one on his shoulder, and holds the babe in his arms. He that could swing a giant and slay him walks about the servant of the little children, so gently that they love him almost more than they love the mother's bosom. It is the sweetness of strength in an element of love that makes gentleness. It is not an attribute of weakness; weakness is not gentle.

I believe in softness in the heart; but I do not believe in having a man's head soft.

There is a great deal of weakness in the world; but that is not gentleness. Soft touches when a man cannot touch any other way than softly, are not gentleness. Gentleness is power, intensity, vigor; power made soft by the sweetness of love is gentleness.

If you would be happy you must do good for the sake of doing good, and not for the sake of the kicking back of happiness on you.

Happiness is just as virtuous as moping melancholy, and a good deal more so.

***

I believe Christ to have been the happiest man that ever dawned above the horizon of time in earthly condition. Do you suppose that such a being exercising the greatest part of a man's nature, his moral nature —bearing in mind that it is more blessed to give than to receive, by His own testimony—do you believe that such a being as He could live in the midst of so much want and trouble, to allay the trouble, staunch the tears, encourage the doubting, heal the sick—do you suppose that He stood and commanded the bier which bore the only son of a widow, and raised him to life, and gave him back to her, and that He stood like an icicle, that He saw it all, and did not feel, did not care? Do you not suppose that even her heart itself could not have had the same exquisite satisfaction that His heart had? When He went to Jarius to raise his daughter, and the sweet maiden came back, and the hearts of the father and mother were melted with joy and gratitude, do you suppose that He had not some sweet thought Who had done all this? Do you suppose that He who raised the dead, gave sight to the blind, wholeness to the lame, purity to the leper— that in all this world of wonder Christ was not happy? I think there was no creature in Palestine so happy as He was.

Let no man tell me that Christ was not a happy man. Listen to the royal sentence—"Who for the joy set before Him, endured the cross, despising the shame, and is set down at the right hand of God." In sorrow are the sweetest elements of joy.

He is called "a man of sorrows and acquainted with grief". He had mighty sorrows, He experienced great grief; but don't tell me Christ was not a happy man.

The body is like a piano, happiness is like music. It is needful to have the instrument in good order. But that is but a beginning. Something must play upon the instrument. And who performs, and from what musical score, will determine the character of the concert. Chickering's grandest piano, with a fool playing jigs on it, is not so good as an old harpsichord with Beethoven at the keys.

If a man has come to that point where he is content, he ought to be put in his coffin; for a contented live man is a shame?

*
* *

Let every man take that which has been given him and be content. God makes sparrows to sing, and they sing as sparrows; he makes bluebirds to sing, and they sing as bluebirds; he makes robins to sing, and they sing as robins; he makes wood-thrushes and larks to sing, and they sing in the way that they were made to sing. They are all parts of the great choir, and each carries his part, and each sings sweeter and better in singing according to his own nature, than he would if he undertook to copy the style of some other bird singer.

* * *

Be content with whatever state you are in — find the right side of it.

* * *

Contentment does not consist in a want of push.

* * *

Once upon a time a little leaf was heard to sigh and cry, as leaves often do when a gentle wind is about. And the twig said, "What is the matter, little leaf?" And the leaf said, "The wind just told me that one day it would pull me off and throw me down to die on the ground!" The twig told it to the branch on which it grew, and the branch told it to the tree. And when the tree heard it, it rustled all over, and sent back word to the leaf, "Do not be afraid; hold on tightly, and you shall not go till you want to". And so the leaf stopped sighing, but went on nestling and singing. Every time the tree shook itself and stirred up all its leaves, the branches shook themselves, and the little twig shook itself, and the little leaf danced up and down merrily, as if nothing could ever pull it off. And so it grew all summer long till October. And when the bright days of autumn came, the little leaf saw all the leaves around becoming very beautiful. Some were yellow, and some scarlet, and some striped with both colors. Then it asked the tree what it meant? And the tree said, "All these leaves are getting ready to fly away, and they have put on these beautiful colors because of joy". Then the little leaf began to want to go, and grew very beautiful in thinking of it, and when it was very gay in color, it saw that the branches of the tree had no color in them, and so the leaf said, "O, branches! why are you lead color and we golden?" "We must keep on our work clothes, for our life is not done; but your clothes are for holiday, because your tasks are over." Just then, a little puff of wind came, and the leaf let go without thinking of it, and the wind took it up, and turned it over and over, and whirled it like a spark of fire in the air and then it fell gently down under the edge of the fence among hundreds of leaves, and fell into a dream and never waked up to tell what it dreamed about.

There are a great many doors open, but a door must be a man's size, or it is not meant for him. I have seen a great many men in for openings that were not for them.

First find out what God has meant you to be — and if you cannot find it out yourself, your friends can very quick — and then enter that department of life for which you were intended.

⁂

How many men that have been bored for forty-pound cannons, have been spoiled in the gun-range!

⁂

No man can do his best work except along the line of his strongest faculties. What if a farmer should harness greyhounds together and plough with them? What if racing on the track was to be made by oxen? An ox is for strength, a greyhound for speed; but men are greyhounds where they ought to be oxen, and oxen where they ought to be greyhounds, all their lives. How should they know? By their blunders mostly. How often most admirable men of ideas are mere copyists! They generate thought, they have latent poetry in them, they have latent inspirations; if they had been put in the right avenues, and under the right inspirations, these men would have been thinkers, and their life like the outpouring of music. One half of the energy of life is badly applied

⁂

It is a great deal better that a man should be a successful carpenter, than that he should be a poor minister of the Gospel. It is a great deal better that a man should be a successful blacksmith than that he should be a drivelling lawyer. Any thing by which you can serve God by your success is respectable.

The church is a garden of the Lord where men are planted for the sake of growing. There is no charm in it, no promise in it; but there is culture, hopefulness and helpfulness in it. Not but that a man may live a Christian life outside of the church — he may. So a man may raise fruit on the side of the road; but the boys will be very apt to steal it; whereas, a sheltered tree behind the wall will carry its fruit to the right hands, and will be permitted to ripen it fully. A man may live a Christian life outside of the church; but he will be an extraordinary man if he does. There are some extraordinary men who do. I do not wish to instill in your minds any superstition that you cannot live a Christian life unless you join the church. You can. A man may go to California across lots if he has a mind to; and if he gets there, he has got there — that is all; but that is not the easiest way, and it is not the way that would be most likely to get him there. A man may educate himself and never go to school; but it is a great deal better that a man should go to school. It will facilitate his learning, and enlarge him in many ways.

Can a man become a Christian without acknowledging Christ? Just as far toward it as an apple can ripen without acknowledging the sun. An apple can grow, and get size, and get shape, and get juice without the shining of the sun; but I will defy any apple to get sweetness out of that juice. I will defy any apple to change its sour sap into sweet sap, until it has the sun shining on it. And no man can become a Christian without the supernal light.

***

You may carry a lighted candle into a conservatory; but it will coax out no blossom. If, however, you let the sun shine in on the plants, a thousand blossoms will come out at once. And there is no mere human element that will ever bring out the blossoms of the soul. You must get the Sun of Righteousness to shine into the soul if you would have it blossom.

***

The spirit of the Gospel is democratic. The tendency of the Gospel is leveling, leveling up — not down. It is carrying the poor and the multitude onward and upward. It is said that democracies have no great men, no heroic men. Why is it so? When you raise the average of intelligence and power in the community it is very hard to be a great man. That is to say, when the great mass of citizens are only ankle high, when among the Lilliputians a Brobdingnagian walks, he is a great man. But when the Lilliputians grow until they get up to his shoulder, he is not so great a man as he was by the whole length of his body. So, make the common people grow, and there is nobody tall enough to be much higher.

The great mistake is made of supposing that an intellectual system is the Gospel. I am sure that there is no Gospel except that which is in the lives of men. The wisdom of God in the production of gentleness, sweetness, patience, long-suffering, disinterestedness and self-sacrifice — that is the Gospel.

Ideas are not Gospel; dispositions are Gospel; and he who brings to men thoughts of liberty in all things right and noble and good, and cheerfulness, and lovableness, and forgiveness, and patience, and long-suffering, and gentleness in the warfare of this life — he that lives Christ knows Christ, and can preach Christ. Nobody else can. You may bring me a catalogue of fruits; all the fruits of earth do not taste good out of a catalogue. Bring me one cluster from the orchard, that touches at once my palate and my imagination. Gospel living is the only ordination that can make a man God's priest and God's minister.

The power of the Gospel is in the living of it, and not in the proclaiming it.

No man can preach any more of the Gospel than he has living in himself.

Sentiments are not despicable because they do not work at the mill, because they do not plow, because they bring no fruit for the counter or the till, because they have no money value. Sentiments are not indifferent and worthless. The riches of life are in them.

People of much sentiment are like fountains, whose overflow keeps a disagreeable puddle about them.

There is a providence of God, of a thinking of God for us; but it is no such providence or thinking as ever takes the place of, or interferes with, our own personal wisdom. There is a providence of God, but it never weaves cloth.

I have noticed that God's providence is on the side of clear heads.

We are the children of the King, and though yet our crown is not stretched out to us, though our hands are too feeble to hold the scepter, we are not unknown wonders in this life. We are well known and thought of, and our names are registered, and our places kept, and all the joy of heaven, that so many myriads possess, is ours.

* * *

The care of no bird that flutters over her nest to feed her young, and the care of no mother who watches the cradle for her babe, is to be compared with God's tender care for us.

* * *

I think the whole round globe is but a cradle, and that God rocks it with his foot.

* * *

God's designs are seeds planted in human affairs — the seed tells the story of its destiny as fast as it grows, no faster.

* * *

God's methods of gaining victories, of securing results, frequently defeat our wisdom. We are in the smoke and confusion of the battle, confused and blinded.

* * *

Like children we like to drive until affairs begin to run away with us; then we cry out, "Where is our Father?"

* * *

God's providence is wiser than man's judgment of his own needs. We are to bear in mind that this life is a mere planting-time. We are started here; we await transplantation through resurrection, and what may seem the neglect of God and a want of providence will reveal itself a step beyond, as being an illustrious Providence, watchful, tender, careful.

* * *

One of the things that makes life endurable is that we are not like so many stones, rolled, broken and rattling down by violent torrents, without any particular force of design; but that we are grouped together in communities and in families; and, as individuals, under the beneficent inspection of God, who has a continual thought of our welfare. The world would seem to me a very dreary place if I did not believe in the immanence of the Divine Mind and the interference of the Divine Will. The belief in a special Divine Providence brings with it great peace and confidence, and is exactly suited to the ignorance and helpless condition of the human race. A chariot with no driver, an engine with no engineer, a voyage and no captain or officers, a raging battle and no commander — what would all these events be in comparison with undirected human life upon this whirling globe, in its endless passage through time, disease, revolution, wars?

* *
*

I plant my hollyhock seeds; and as the season goes on I see that they were good seeds, and that they are all coming up. I rejoice in them. I take them up, in due time, and transplant them to beds where, separated, they shall have a chance of root-room and nourishment and growth. Later I go and look at them, and by that time I find that they are all crested with leaves. As they do not blossom the first year, I take them up and put them where I want them. The next spring I look at them again. Winter has not killed them. All is going right, with good soil, good roots, good leaves; and they are beginning to throw up the important central stem, and it goes on and up and up. Finally the buds begin to appear. Then comes some blundering man with hoe or hand, and cuts off the top; and they do not grow further. Now, was not the root a very good thing? Were not the basilar leaves very good things? Was not the central stem a very good thing as far as it went? But when it was cut off you did not get any blossoms, did you? You lost the whole thing for which you had planted your hollyhocks. You had no blossoms, the end for which you planted.

So, a man says, "Why, I have got up as far as morality." What then? You have got as far as morality, and that is as high as you have gone. You have not come to buds and blossoms. If you change the figure from a hollyhock to a vine, you certainly have not come to fruit. It is a desirable thing to have

a good root, but you cannot do anything with that
alone. It is a very desirable thing that every root
should have a stem, but what are you going to do with
it? It is very desirable that the stem should have
blossoms; but if a frost comes and cuts off your blossoms what are you going to do for grapes? You have
lost the very thing for which you planted your vineyard. Yet all the way up each particular step was
important.

* * *

Morality is the beginning of spirituality. No spiritual element ever existed without a foundation of
morality. I have just been beholding with fresh delight the achievements of the magnolia, which in
spring carries at its very top the bright white cup, as if
it were filled with the very ether and essence of sunlight and fragrance. And yet that cup, holding itself
so, is dependent on that homely, dirt-colored root at
the bottom. Destroy the root and you will destroy
the cup. All the way from the bottom clear up to the
top there is this perfect unity of organization and
evolvement, and as the sweet censer of fragrance and
beauty in the tree is intimately connected with its root,
so morality and spirituality are one, only at different
stages and positions of growth.

* * *

Morals bear to spirituality the same relation which
the root bears to the blossom and the fruit. We have

been taught that morality will not avail us, and that spirituality is the only saving element; whereas, there is no spirituality itself without morality; all true spirituality is an out-growth, it is the blossom and fruit on the stem of morality.

*
* *

What is a revival of religion? It is simply a phenomenon in common with a multitude of others in variety, by which the feelings of men gather strength by the collected and connected feelings in the same direction of the multitudes in society. It is easy to do business when business rushes and everybody is in the market; it is easy to be patriotic when the whole community is roused to that one current of thought. Fashion becomes very catching indeed when everybody is bent upon this superlative quality; the run of the mind is helped by the run of other minds in the same direction. Now when revivals of religion are "got up", as it is said, it is simply a natural bringing together of men, and by teaching and singing, bringing their thoughts into the same channel until one with another they coalesce, and the fire is kindled and it flows on, and the man finds himself segregated from his old companions and habits, and he finds it is easier to turn his thoughts to religion and the purposes of reformation than it would be if he stood alone. It is hard to make one brand burn itself out, but put plenty together and you kindle a fire that consumes them all. There is no reason, therefore, why there should not be these methods in religion which we denominate "revivals", applying to the highest things of life that which we are accustomed to apply to all the fundamental and lower developments of human society.

＊

As God gives a great seed-time, and a great and general harvest, to every year, and yet fills up the months with incidental and perpetual blossoming and ripening of some sweet thing; so he gives to every true and intelligent church constant budding, constant blossoming. But, besides that, in grander profusion — there is the greater harvest, in which the whole year opens its bosom and exhibits its vast richness! There may be a harvest of cockles and chess, but that does not argue against true wheat or corn! There may be an autumn for the crab-tree and the bitter sloe, but that does not take from the glory of the orchard, nor from the exquisite flavor of its superabundant fruits. There may be ascetic revivals, and revivals corrupted to mere zeal; but there are also healthful revivals, sweet-hearted, full of love and joy, whose fruit is fragrant and wholesome, as if plucked from the tree of life in the garden of God.

＊

Revivals of religion and all kinds of religious service in churches, that melt, lift, and inspire men to a higher life, are normal. No science is going to abolish them. You might as well put icicles under your kettle to get boiling water, as to put scientific problems about electricity under the church to get lukewarmness boiling and evaporating.

***

A single candle throws light to one man who reads, and only one. A hundred candles give light to every man in the house. A single stick does not create much warmth; a fagot more; a bonfire more yet; and a furnace melts all things in its glow and heat. A single penitent thought limps; a thousand men, all of them feeling the pressure of wrongdoing in the past, and the desire for elevation and inspiration, reflect their feeling one upon the other, and it becomes easy for each to do that which it would otherwise be almost impossible to do.

***

There can be no mode, however sacred, by which the new birth can be administered officially from without. It is simply a natural part of the unfolding series designed of God in the human constitution; an illustration of that transcendent doctrine, that when a man has unfolded through the lower and intermediate stages, however wise, however useful, however humble, however good, there is in all these things no reason why he should not rise higher, and evolve from those lower preparatory stages into the higher and spiritual stages and instincts of the human mind. Conversion is part and parcel of this grand idea of unfolding.

When there dawns upon the human soul a conception of supernal grandeur in power and illumination in wisdom — a conception of that Nature whose love is most exquisite, passing the love of woman, passing a lover's love, passing the love of a mother, in length and breadth and intensity; when from the heavens above and around there comes to a human soul the conception that there is a Being with soul attributes, and the soul knows it, and is waked by it, as the cloud knows how to wake when the sun comes; when the human soul, having gained such a conception of God, begins to move, and to be filled and intensified by hope and faith and love, and to be wound up and kept in order thereby; when in this way God's love through Jesus Christ comes into the soul — then that soul is born again, re-created, without anything being added to it, simply by having that which belongs to it regulated, trained, stimulated, washed, and made in spiritual things effluent and beautiful as angels are.

All ordinances are for the individual Christian who needs Christ.

Who shall partake of this Lord's Supper? They that need something in life to help them; they that need an inspiration to grow better; they that need some help to break off easily besetting sins; they that need to have stability infused into their changeable purposes; they that are in a fight with their selfishness, and avarice, pride, and want a Leader, a Captain of salvation; they that are in sorrow and trouble, and want a Comforter; all men that have distresses for which God is a physician. They are called. Only do not feign; do not come through superstition; come through trust and faith that this sets forth an all-helping Saviour. If you need help, come.

Dogma is indispensable to religion, but it must be in its place.

Ordinances are nothing unless they serve the weaknesses of men. If a man can get along without them better than with them, he is at liberty to do it; but in dispensing with them he is not to despise religion; for religion does not consist in being a member of a church, or reciting the catechism, or repeating so much Scripture; it is a living quality in the living man. It is the right exercise of right feelings all the time, toward God and toward men.

Ordinances are not to be despised, unless you put them in the place of God; they are not to be despised if they lead you up to God, and so vacate themselves. A ladder is a thing that a man must leave every round of, or else he will not get to the top. If a man takes just one step on the ladder, and stops there and roosts, the ladder is of no account to him; the rounds of the ladder are things to be left behind or below. Multitudes of men there are that are so busy looking at the rounds of the ladder that they do not see the angels at all up there; they are looking down to see if they are stepping right.

* * *

After a long drought when the earth is athirst we do not say, "O rain! fill my cup", and another, "O rain! fill my barrel". The God-ordained clouds march in grandeur through the heavens, they drop down their treasures freely, constantly, overflowingly, all through the day and through the night. They rain according to the multitude of the drops they contain in themselves, not according to the size of the cup you hold out. We hold out our little silver cup and with strong importunity cry out, "O Lord, bless me so much!" and God is ready to bestow according to the fullness of his infinite nature.

All earthly symbols stop far this side of the abundance of God's goodness in the kingdom of grace. And this is above all human aspirations or desires· Consider how much men do ask; in times when love makes the heart full as mountains make the streams in spring. What a wondrous literature is there in the prayers of exiles alone, what heart throes, and yearnings. Yet the bounty of God is above all that has ever been asked. But who does not know that there is more within the lips than ever comes out of them. Who, then, can measure what the soul "thinks"—the flights of aspiration, the wishes, the yearnings for itself and even more for others. Yet after we have done the mightiest things thought, the highest felt the deepest, all that we have thought, or felt, or done, is but as the drop of dew upon the grass, in comparison with the ocean of God's goodness.

If you had the art to gather up all the sunbeams flashing through space, gilding every man, illumining the ice pallaces of the poles and burning in the luxuriance of the tropics, falling thro' the whole bright air in its liquid torrent, filling every flower-cup, resting on every blade of grass, gleaming on the prisoner's window, and gilding the fetters of the slave, glorifying the humblest things and the highest—the sunlight in its wild abundance, ever since creation began, pouring its full, fresh, overflowing tide, you would then have God's own figure of the boundless copiousness of his compassion—its inexhaustibleness, its application to every possible phase of human life.

How strange that the most wonderful views of the Divine compassion are from Moses, and David the warrior-king. Noble old warrior! Thy arrows turned not back, mighty ones fell beneath thy sword, but those silver shafts of song drawn from a quiver beyond Apollo's, pierce the heart not to slay but to heal. Like beams of sunlight they shine across the ages, filling the hearts of nations with life and light and joy.

* * *

O, how easy dost Thou forgive and forget! As the waters cover the sands, so Thy love our barrenness. As the very waves forget their tempest-tossed condition, so Thou speakest to our troubled souls and darkness flies, and tumult.

* * *

Lord, we need Thy compassion every day, we are so unstable; our vision is often fugitive, we so frequently forget. Some days Thou dost lift us upon the Mount of Transfiguration, and all is divine, and we marvel at our unbelief, and fain would abide in those heights of joy and trust; and yet ere one day is passed how low the light has descended, and how feeble is the pulse, and how are we quickly turned to doubting, to fear or to irresolution! We discern the right way, but how are we to follow? How often our very best followings lead us astray! How often are we conquered by that which should give us victory!

* * *

If God wants you to work, work; but work out your

true manhood. If He wants you to stand, stand; but stand in your true manhood. If He wants you to lie down, lie down; but, lying down, let your true manhood shine out.

* * *

This world is a world of anvils, of benches, of plows, of looms, of everything which indicates that men must work out their own salvation. *Work* may be said to be the birth-cry of creation to every man that comes into the world.

* * *

Men must not plant over night and think they will reap the crop next morning. When men undertake any work, which involves the judgment of men and the conscience of men and the hearts of men, great patience is necessary, that they may in due season reap what they have sown.

* * *

They need no monuments whose lives have been so fruitful that the result of their living is known and read of all men. When we pronounce their names, it is the opening of the door of history. Up springs to thought the representative influences set in motion and the deeds performed by them.

***

If you would work easily never let your work drive you.

***

Men work; their whole life is a series of earnest labors; and when they die they seem to themselves to have done very little; for no man makes any account of the secondary influences which he exerts; no man makes any account of what he stirs other people up to do; no man makes any account of the work that he commences, but that is to be finished by future generations. Men very seldom understand that that which they begin, and which they carry forward to a certain point, will inevitably fall into other hands and be consummated by them. There are multitudes of men whose minds have been the leaven of the age in which they lived; but dying, they seem to have done very little. They do not own houses and lands; they have no bank stock. They seem not to have done much; but after all, dying, dead, their works follow them; and men who come after them say, "The whole magnitude of these results flowed from them".

***

God says to some, "Work", to others, "Wait". If you are whelmed and whirled in the fury of battle, serve God there; or if wounded and disabled you are dragged away from the scene of action, say, "Lord, is it here Thou wouldst have me? Here then I wish to be."

* * *

The question is not how much have you been able to do, but how completely have you done what you could. All God requires is that the whole soul be put to use.

Prose is the work-day dress in which truths do secular duty. Poetry is the robe, the royal apparel, in which truth asserts its Divine origin. Prose is truth looking on the ground; eloquence is truth looking up to heaven; poetry is truth flying upward toward God.

* * *

I believe in foreign missions. I believe that they have their best results, however, at home. The old musket was far more effectual at the butt than it was at the muzzle, and the kick-back of the education which leads us to go out into all the world to preach the Gospel elevates the standard of devotion in our home churches; and I think our home churches are more profited than the heathen ones, although they are helped.

Christianity is the science of right living. It is the new manship of the world.

* * *

Whatever elements go to make men deeper, higher, wider; whatever enlarges man's horizon; whatever makes him an heir of two worlds, and worthy to be made king, not by an outward crown but by a crown of the heart; whatever makes him more like God, and more deserving of the love of God — all of that belongs to Christianity; and the unexpressed part of Christianity is a thousand times more than that which has been expressed.

Christianity is the alphabet, and life is the literature which springs from that alphabet.

Let men search for hidden records — for the footsteps of God on the Globe. Let men make discoveries in the stellar depths. Let men develop new economies and philosophies. Let men open up other realms of knowledge. Let whatever there may be in the sphere of human society be disclosed. It does not follow that it is not in harmony with religion because it is not a part of that which is hereditary and conventional. Christianity in its nature is interminable, universal, unfathomable. That belongs to Christianity, which is sanctified, divine manhood in men.

* * *

The man that knows God's laws in the world and conforms to them, has God in him, working for him. I cannot grind as the old mill did, but I can make a river do it for me; I cannot control the elements, but electricity can fix them so that they run across the ocean, and can make them light cities. If anybody who understands God's law obeys it, that law turns round and says, "Well, stranger, what do you want? I will do it for you". Obedience to Divine law is liberty, power, satisfaction.

* * *

The law of creation is that the higher forms of development require more labor than the lower. Religious life becomes more difficult in proportion as it comes up higher. It is not very hard for a woodsman to cut down a tree. There are many who cut a tree down in a day. It is not very hard for the mill owner to saw it up. The old saw rips through it and sings all day long. It is not very hard for a man to bring it up into the shop and cut out the rough furniture. When it is cut up the difficulty grows, and a little more as it is cut cut and as the fitting comes; and when the fitting and the rough dressing are over, then begin to come the real difficulties. It has got to go through the finer processes, and the last hand that puts the last touch of beauty and polish upon it is the rarest hand in the whole force. There are five hundred men that can do rough cabinet work where there is one man that can do the artistic and finer cabinet work. That is true of every department of human life. It is easy to begin those things, but the difficulties increase. It is often said, when men speak of the crowded state of things and the difficulty of getting along, "There is room at the top". There is always room at the top, but the difficulty is in getting there. There is always room at the top for learning. As you go on in life the difficulties increase, of finer justice, of a finer sense of love, of a finer sense of propriety, of a finer sense of effluence that comes from the high development of all the faculties, of a finer sense of the irradiation of a noble life, of a finer sense of forbearance and self-denying, of a finer sense of being under the active influence in the forthgoing of the energies and faculties that tend to make heroic, Christian manhood. These difficulties increase; and I think a true man of God never feels so little like a true man as when he is nearest like it. The sense of that which remains to be accomplished is greater than the sense of that which has been attained.

All real laws that are beneficial to human society are God's laws. They may be enacted at Albany or Washington, and the very enactors may in themselves not be specially dignified nor worthy of our particular confidence; but where law gathers up usage, where law authenticates what has already been demonstrated by experiment, and gives to it the sanction of the universal judgment and conscience, that law is Divine. It is Divine no matter whether it touches a man's body, or his intellect, or his soul. There is relative importance or gradation of importance in it, but whether it touches men nearly or remotely, it is a Divine moral law.

* * *

A man who is just as good as the law makes him is a mean man.

* * *

Laws depend upon human intelligence for their achievements. In their wildest state natural laws are only half fruitful. Winds have roamed like wild giants over the globe, roaring hither and thither, before there was a human population; but now they grind the food of man by turning windmills, or swell the sails that carry men for all their purposes round and round the world. The wild wind that knew no master is apprenticed to ten thousand masters to-day. Human reason has taken possession of it and made it work for its living. Water floated in the clouds or stormed on the sea, or rushed forth in useless rivers. It, too, has been reduced to service, everywhere turning wheels, everywhere replenishing the supplies of society through the medium of manufactories; and even in the desert, by irrigation, making the wilderness to bud and blossom as the rose. Water had never done that of itself; water inspired by human will does it.

Electricity, the great buffoon of the North in winter nights, flashes, too, in storms — the pyrotechnist of the world. But to-day it is subdued. Now, shut up in boxes, it heals the sick. It lights our streets and dwellings. It plays post-boy and carries news in the twinkling of an eye around the whole world. In its early day, untouched by the will of man, what did the electric element do? It was worthless, barren, fruitless, or fruitful only of harm to the works of man; and it became very fruitful to all functions of good simply because the will of man learned to utilize it.

Not by violating, either, but by using the laws of Nature, men can and do create a providence; and thus we come back to the gist of the matter. I can use the laws of Nature so that they shall be a providence to me, and I can use them so that they shall be a providence to my family.

* * *

In proportion as things are complex, and work toward fine results, delay is characteristic of them. If you look at the seasons, you find that there are some things which, early in the spring, rush right up with the first relaxation of the winter, develop themselves and come to an end.

There are many things — for instance, the asters, and the chrysanthemums — which grow all summer long, and do not look out with rosy blossoms upon you until just before the frost cuts them down. There are many things which grow all summer long, and which, when the winter finds them, have not done their duty, or at any rate their work; and it is not until the end of another summer that they show forth the nature that is in them. And then there are a great many things which neither in one year, nor in two years, nor in twenty years, show what they are. They require more time for their development. You can grow a head of lettuce in the space of six weeks; but you cannot grow a hollyhock in less than two years; and you cannot grow an oak tree in fifty years.

To make an old-fashioned loom was not a very laborious thing; one could almost hew it out with an ax; but to make a power loom is a very different thing. No man can do that with one tool nor with twenty. The one could be built in a few days; the other requires months in which to be built. The difference lies in the greater convenience of the latter, in its complexity, and in the excellence of the results which it is expected to work out.

When you want low things, common things, you can have them quick; but if you want high and good things, you must wait for them.

It is a great thing to know how to work; it is also a great thing to know how to wait. It is very easy for some persons to know how to be energetic and enterprising; but they know also how to be irritable and impatient when energy and enterprise do not speedily bring the fruit which they are after. To know how to work, and to know just as well how to wait; to have all the drive of enterprise, and besides, to have undomitable patience in waiting for the fruit of enterprise — this is to be a completed man — a true workman of God.

They are of as much worth whom God is holding in

reserve, as those who at the front of the battle do the actual fighting.

* * *

It matters not if men roll my name about in slanderous reports, as a boy would roll a foot-ball down a dirty street, so long as the cause of God succeeds.

* * *

But is the gate out of which hell comes; and *If* is the other leaf of that gate, for it is a double-leaved one. If and but have destroyed more souls than any fiend in hell.

* * *

A man who with open eye and clear understanding permits wrong to be done without protest and without resistance up to the measure of his power, has responsibility for the sum total of all that wrong. If in a partnership two, three, or four men proceed upon a deliberately dishonest method of conducting business, and one man knowing that it is wrong, is peaceable, the responsibility is his. Nobody has a right to be peaceable when there is sin around, and when it is surrounding him. If there is this wrong doing he cannot say to himself, "There are four partners and I shall only have about a fourth part of this responsibility". You have the whole of it! God does not make dividends in those things.

I hate a man built on the pattern of a wasp, beautiful all the way down, with all his forces centered in a sting.

* * *

Many a man will steal or embezzle, for years, and never once call it by the right name — never! If he happen to say to himself, "I am a thief", he will spring back as if God had spoken to him; it is like poison to him. "Thief!" I don't believe you could make many men steal in that way; but financiering is a very different thing. Call it "stealing?" Oh, no; call it an arrangement. Call it "thieving?" Oh, no; call it an unfortunate affair. Call it "robbery?" Oh, no; an unfortunate mistake. We talk about bandaging our eyes, but I think men bandage their eyes with their mouths oftener than in any other way.

* * *

A fit speech is like a sweet and favorite tune. Once struck out it may be sung or played forever. It flies from man to man, and makes its nest in the heart as birds do in trees.

* * *

The tongue is the key-board of the soul. But it makes a world of difference who sits to play upon it.

***

The tongue of man cannot be described. It has deep and inward relations. It has national and political bearings. It is the silver bell of the soul, or the iron and crashing hammer of the anvil. It is like a magician's wand, full of all incantation and witchery; or it is a sceptre in a king's hands and sways with imperial authority.

***

There never has been yet upon the face of this earth, under any kingdom, in any period, anywhere, such an exhibition of submission to the Divine will as has been shown by the slaves of America. There were four millions of men during our war that knew just as well as their masters did that this was a war either for slavery or for liberty; they were couched down in the families of their masters, and the Southern armies had drafted almost every able-bodied man away from the plantations and away from the villages, and the land was really in the power of the Africans that were left at home; they knew their wrongs, they knew that their children had been sold from their arms; they knew that they lived in darkened huts and cottages, deprived of the elements of civilization; they were sensitive to it; and yet during that whole period of five years there was never a record made of cruelty on the part of the slaves to the helpless families of their masters. There never was an insurrection during that period in all the length and breadth of the

Southern States. Prayers there were, and singing and tears for deliverance, and faith in God that the day was coming and that they were to be free; but they sat down in perfect patience and in fidelity to their masters during that great struggle. If there ever were men, by multitudes, by millions, that fulfilled the Apostolic command to be faithful to those that were their masters in the Lord, it was the American slaves.

Everywhere, the best heroes in the world are those that have no trumpets blared before them. After times will praise them.

It is only so much of Christ as we carry to heaven, that will make us heroes there.

It is not doing great things that constitutes heroism; it is not doing brilliant things; it is doing things which indicate an appreciation of a higher manhood.

Occasions do not make heroes; they merely develop them. Where it is shown it belongs to a man, and it merely flashes out upon occasion.

Do not think that conspicuity is necessary to heroism. Only now and then is a gold vein found and brought to light; but the mountains are full of gold veins. Only now and then is a pearl found and worn; but there are myriads of pearls hidden in oysters beneath the waters of the sea. And there are many heroes obscured by coverings as homely as the oyster; and when God makes up his jewels, not one of them shall be left out. Do not say, "Nobody will know it if I am heroic". Yes; somebody will know it whose touch is immortality, whose love is better than ownership of the round world, and who has reserved for you a life higher than that of the body, nobler than that of the flesh.

***

It is a glorious thing to have a freshet in the soul! To have the better feelings overflow their banks and carry out of the channel all the dull obstructions of ordinary life. It reveals us to ourselves. It augments the sense of being. In these higher moods of feeling there is intuitional moral instruction, to the analysis of which the intellect comes afterward with slow steps.

***

There is but one first time to anything; and he is foolish indeed that squanders it by giving himself to analysis, instead of yielding himself to sympathy and enthusiasm; and the more artless and unashamed his enjoyment, the better. Pleasure and inspiration first, analysis afterward.

When a man has in him the consciousness that this life is but the prelude — is but the morning star of existence, the sunrise of His might — when we believe that the Divine Spirit is diffused through all things in this world — God is everywhere, above, below, either side, impending, universal, constant, and continuous; when we live in Him as men live in sunshine — when a man is in that state of mind, and all his thoughts are heavenward, or else earthward for the groanings of the captives that they may be delivered — when a man lives in that state and it becomes his necessary life, his joy and his enthusiasm, such a life as that cannot be a barren one in the flesh.

A dull, watery, sluggish brain may do for a Conservative; but God never made them to be fathers of progress. They are very useful as brakes on the wheel down hill; but they never would draw anything up hill in the world.

Strong natures, strong enough to overturn old errors, and fight great battles, are likely to be too strong to walk safely in harness and drag our phaetons and chaises.

Those who look with fear and suspicion upon enthusiasm agree not with the teaching of God. Many are inclined to suspect those who have a momentum of goodness, they think where there is growth there is danger of rankness. The danger of poverty and barrenness is more to be feared. If people felt about spiritual poverty as they do about temporal poverty we should have more and better Christians. No man can become a Christian without being in some degree an enthusiast, though persons differ in this respect in original temperament. A heart deepened and enriched by the love of Christ flows over and over beyond possibility of measurement. The kingdom of God is not in the head but the heart.

No man can understand God by the intellect; no man can understand God by any ratiocinative process. But He that is filled with the afflatus of love knows and feels God, just as a man knows when it is summer without looking in his almanac; God is in him, round about him, above him, below him.

Sin is of the will; infirmity is of ignorance and weakness. Men have not learned how to use the faculties which in ascending gradations demand vast experience. It is the richness of human nature that confuses man and makes duty so difficult. Shall the hand require long practice before it works skilfully and achieves success, and the mind not demand time, culture, practice, before it can work harmoniously within itself, and amid the external distractions of social and civil life? Men are responsible for sin, but not for infirmity. Infirmities are the mistakes which men make on their way to knowledge. Life is a trade, to be learned; a profession, to be gained by education; an art, requiring long drill. Man must learn his trade —the most complex, the most subtle, and the most difficult that ever was learned. No man learns it except by help of institutions, by public sentiment, by direct moral influences, brought to bear upon him. The education of a man should unfold his nature in harmony with himself, in harmony with his fellows, in harmony with God. The knowledge of how a man shall ascend from the control of his animal instincts requires a training, an education, that is not learned in a day, and was learned by the race only through slow-creeping centuries.

If I say, "You have inherited from Adam a corrupt nature", you may justly rise up and say, "I have not; I inherited from my father and mother as pure a nature as ever descended to a child. There has no drop of Adam's bad blood come through to me." But if I say to you, "God has made man a progressive creature, beginning at the very bottom, on the line of the material, first the animal, then the social, then the intellectual, the æsthetic, the spiritual; and every one of you should live so as to travel on and up. But you have not done it; you are living in the lower portions of your nature; you are not acting becomingly to yourself or your Creator"—if I say this, there is not a man who can or will deny it. The doctrine of sin, as reflected in the philosophy of Evolution, will carry more power, and have more effect upon the conscience and the aspirations of men, and upon the desires for a higher and better life, than any other. It will explain to them the road by which they are to travel, and the directions they are to take, away from appetites and passions, and will enable them to live more and more perfectly in the higher ranges of emotion and moral sensibility.

* * *

Adam's sin was his own, and no one else's. It never descended. There is none of it in all the world. No immersion, effusion or sprinkling does any infant need to cleanse from Adam's sin. A single drop is enough for the whole world and for all ages. A microscope of ten thousand million power, in examining the infant soul, could not magnify and bring into vision one single solitary speck of anything Adam did or did not do.

* * *

The old theology makes sin to spring from a corrupt nature. I make it spring from a nature not corrupted, but not unfolded nor harmoniously developed. Both Evolution and the New Testament show that sin springs from the struggle for the relative ascendency of animal and spiritual in man's double nature, and that the conflicts of life are simply the conflicts between the lower and upper man.

* * *

Sin is a term that applies to the act of violated law; and whoever purposely violates a known law sins. If he violates laws not known to him, or without deliberation, it is infirmity; but all sin is simply the act of the sinner, and it must have the element of voluntariness in it, or it ceases to be sin. All the doctrines that speak about sins as a kind of soot in the channels of a man, in the flues, as it were, of his life, as hereditary sins, or as imputed sins, are a part of the pagan nightmare of mediæval theology. Whoever does wrong, knowing that he does, and for a purpose, sins; whoever neglects a duty, and knows it is duty, sins. The purpose, affirmatively or negatively violating God's law, is sinning.

* * *

It has come down in the catechisms and in the creeds of Christianity not only that our first parents fell by their transgression, but that in consequence of their fall the curse passed upon the whole human family, and that there has not been a man made right from that day to this. What sort of a god do you present, then? If in the fall of the family the consequences rested upon them that transgressed, we should have no legal objection to such a sentence; but to say that the unborn millions that had no part nor lot in the transgression of our first parents were to suffer degradation and annihilation, as it were, in consequence of a sin that they never committed nor gave any consent to is to establish an idea of justice that would turn heaven into tyranny and God into a malefactor.

But that is not the worst of it. That after such an imputation of sin that men knew nothing about, God should have gone on and turned the crank of creation, and multiplied them, and multiplied them, and multiplied them, swarming the earth with them in every generation — why, what would you think of a doctor who should go about inoculating men with maddogism, in this world? How long would you let him stay? How long would you let a man with small-pox wander up and down? But suppose a man were to create it, and should be suffered to go into society! All the instincts of justice, all the humanities, rise up against the continued creation of inevitable and unbounded evil.

We often speak of the folly of those who, inheriting an old estate with grand old trees of a century's growth, whose majestic arches of boughs and massive foliage diffuse a perpetual twilight coolness, level these monarchs with the dust — and then when the heats of summer come bethink themselves of shade, and forthwith set out little shadowless sticks — such is the folly of those who forsake the shadow of the tree of life, for the miserable shade of their own hands' planting.

Men seem to think that they have to wait till there is some feeling given to them before they can repent.

How much wind does a vessel need to get out of harbor? A tornado? A gale? A fresh, strong-blowing breeze? Open your sails, and if there is nothing but a zephyr, if it swells the sail and gives steerage way, and you can go slowly out the harbor, you have wind enough; you might do better with more, but this will answer your purpose.

Our Saviour is forever saying to men, "Let me help you"—and the moment a man wants to be helped, and says to Christ, "Help me", the work has begun in him.

Repentance is difficult only to a low and mean spirit. Where wrong has been committed acknowledgment and amendment is a necessity to a noble nature. It is the triumph of the generous feelings over the worse and meaner ones.

*
* *

When a man defers becoming a Christian deliberately to the end of life, saying to himself, "I will get all the pleasure there is in life first, and then, at the end of life, I will take a turn and save myself"—such a man is a sneak; he is a cowardly fellow, a dishonorable man, and Satan outwits him nine times out of ten. The hour of weakness, when the eye is clouded and the world is reeling, is not the hour for one to make that great vow and dedication of himself and of his powers to God. "Ah, but the thief on the cross —he was converted, was he not?" I think he was saved, but I think he had a good many awkward years after he got in Paradise before he knew how to behave himself even decently, and a man must be low down on the scale when he takes a thief for his example.

Hard as it is to transplant the tree of your soul, difficult as it is to sever the roots that hold it down, the Master says, "There is power to do it". However many faults you may have, that branch their roots out in every direction, and difficult as it is to transplant them by ordinary instrumentalities; nevertheless, faith in the soul will give you power to pluck them up by the roots, and cast them from you, or transplant them to a better soil, where they will grow to a better purpose.

O, fool! O, double fool! You who insure your ships by sea, and your warehouses by land; you who guard yourselves and your gold, your bonds and you"

mortgages, but leave your souls exposed in peril to all the wiles and influences of the world! With no insurance, and with no hope, without God and without hope in the world, are you not a double fool? Is it not time to cease your folly and begin to be wise? If you are going to begin, why not to-day? And if to-day, why not now? And if now, why not in the very solitude of your soul accept Christ who says, "I stand at the door and knock". Open the door, and say to him, "By Thy help I will live for Thee".

I do not believe in the old stiff, ledger-like account of a man's conduct, so that just so many sins are set down against him, and just so many virtues are set down to his credit. I believe the soul's life with God is like the child's life with the mother. Do you suppose, when a child has a great, true-hearted mother, that she keeps an account of all its imperfections? Do not you know that she pours over the child such a flood of love that, though its life is not perfect, though its whole being is imperfect, yet through sympathy and kindness and forgiveness, she accepts it with complacency, as though it were perfect? And I believe the soul rises into such a communion with God that, though in its relations to time and space it may be subject to a thousand imperfections and discords, yet those imperfections and discords are overlooked and excused by God's great love. When I walked one day on the top of Mount Washington (glorious day of memory! Such another day I think I shall not experience till I stand on the battlements of the New Jerusalem) how I was discharged of all imperfection! The wide, far-spreading country which lay beneath me in beauteous light—how heavenly it looked! And I communed with God. I had sweet tokens that He loved me. My very being rose right up into His nature. I walked with Him. And cities far and near—New York, and all cities and villages that lay between it and me—with their thunder; the wranglings of human passions below me, were to me as if they were not. Standing as I did, high above them, it seemed to me as though they did not exist. There were the attritions, and cruel grindings, and cries and tears, and shocks of the human life below, but I was lifted up so high that they were nothing to me. The sounds died out, and I was lost with God. And the mountain-top was never so populous to me as when I was absolutely alone.

So it is with the soul that goes up into the bosom of Christ. There is a reach where the arrows of envy cannot strike you. There is a reach where not even your sins can annoy you. Your soul may so rise into the bosom of God that your personal self shall seem annihilated. What you are you are by the grace of God. You may receive such an influx of the life of God that you shall seem to yourself perfect.

Do not suppose that that man is a Christian that

has a poetic and dramatic experience, and you are not one because you have only a drudging journey which, with muddy shoes, you are seeking to perform. When a man is on the road, and slips up or falls down, he does not turn round and go home saying, "I will not journey". He plucks himself up, and shakes his garments, and goes on. You may be a very poor Christian, probably you are — we all of us are — but at every stumble, and lapse, and everything that reveals to us how low we are down yet on the scale, take courage; you have got God for you; He is on your side, and all the universe may be on the other side and it won't amount to that. Who can harm us if God be for us? "Who can separate us from the love of Christ?"

I was a child of teaching and prayer; I was reared in the household of faith; I knew the Catechism as it was taught; I was instructed in the Scriptures as they were expounded from the pulpit, and read by men; and yet, till after I was twenty-one years old, I groped without the knowledge of God in Christ Jesus. I know not what the tablets of eternity have written down, but I think that when I stand in Zion and before God, the brightest thing which I shall look back upon will be that blessed morning of May, when it pleased God to reveal to my wandering soul the idea that it was His nature to love a man in his sins for the sake of helping him out of them; that He did not do it out of compliment to Christ, or to a law, or to a plan of salvation, but from the fullness of His great heart; that He was a Being not made mad by sin, but sorry; that He was not furious with wrath toward the sinner, but pitied him — in short, that He felt toward me as my mother felt toward me, to whose eyes my wrong doing brought tears, who never pressed me so close to her as when I had done wrong, and who would fain, with her yearning love, lift me out of trouble. And when I found that Jesus Christ had such a disposition, and that when His disciples did wrong, He drew them closer to Him than He did before — that when pride, and jealousy, and rivalry, and all vulgar and worldly feelings rankled in their bosoms, He opened His heart to them as a medicine to heal these infirmities; when I found that it was Christ's nature to lift men out of weakness to strength, out of impurity to goodness, out of everything low and debasing to superiority, I felt that I had found a God. I shall never forget the feelings with which I walked forth that May morning. The golden pavements will never feel to my feet as then the grass felt to them.

All natures come to their manhood through some experience of fermentation! With some, it is a ferment of passions; with some, of the affections; and with richly endowed natures it is the ferment of thought and of the moral nature.

We seek the highest peaks if we wish the widest

view. When God takes you by the hand and leads you up on the mountain of some peculiar experience and is transfigured before you, remember that vision, it may never return. Precisely the same experience is never repeated. There are times when the Sun of Righteousness is specially near in times of affliction, but men bow down their heads. The very time when God meant that we should see his inner nature and feel the pulse of his mighty government is spent in weeping and wiping of eyes. It is the time to lift up the head and attend to the revelation of God.

There never will be two experiences exactly alike until you get two men exactly alike.

He that has come under the controlling influence of love to God and to man, and feels it every day, need not disturb himself and trouble his conscience how he got there. If he is there he is there. Do you not believe the sun rises? You saw it yesterday morning come up over the horizon clear and radiant from the moment it struck the atmosphere. To-morrow it comes up under a cloud; it is noonday before you see the sun, but the sun rose then. And the Sun of Righteousness rises to some behind clouds, but to others in a clear sky; it rises if the fruits of righteousness are developed in the conscience and the life.

Don't wait for ideal experiences. Begin where you are.

Our moral experiences are flashes. Would that they were such flashes as lighthouses give, which revolve at times with diminished and extinguished light, only the more to make emphasis with the renewed gleam on the eye of him who, afar off at sea, is reading the signs and tokens of the shore. Men do not intermit their experiences in this way. They let the fire go out.

Conscience is a good thing when it works in sunshine and love, but when it works in acerbity conscience is a bull-dog that sits at the door and keeps out less mischief than it lets in.

One of the saddest effects in connection with the institutions of Christianity—not Christianity itself—has been that the line of their march has been a line of skulls and bones and blood, and the music of their progress has been sighs and weepings and sorrows. It has been clashing, quarreling, fighting; for let me tell you, that when the battle is set upon the conscience, there is no such battle as that known in this whole world. Let a body of men think that God has inspired them above everybody else — nay, laid on them the duty to declare and call men to believe certain things; and let another body be called at just the opposite side, both of them called of God, both of them raising big conscience, both of them defending the faith that was given to the saints, and history shows that there is no such quarrelsomeness on the face of the earth. Conscience is a good thing, conscience in love; but conscience in hate is the very devil of ecclesiasticism.

* * *

That man is a *roué* whose conscience is to let, and who runs equally well under all circumstances, and with all sorts of conduct.

* * *

There is what might be called the microscopic conscience — it is a conscience that concerns itself principally about minute things, none for broad, large views, has no momentum in it, no trusting of itself, without which a man is but a poor creature — invertebrate. A man ought to have a stride, not a pit-a-pat step, and there are multitudes of persons that are looking at little bits of things all the day long, little events going before and going behind, but in no large movement in right directions trusting themselves. I hold that as it is with the rail-car, so it is with the ship, when once the motion is impelled the momentum is of vast importance. And in society a man that is all the time stopping to see whether he is doing right or not, and analyzing his thoughts and his motives and his feelings without any knowledge of how to analyze; the man that is anxious because he did not know but he may have said something to-day; he is like a man that is so anxious that he stops his watch every few minutes to see whether it is going.

A great many men have a conscience for Sunday, but none for Monday.

Oftentimes a text is like a gate which the children love to swing on, but at other times a text is that gate through which you go into the great fields beyond, and use it and pass on.

Build up such a spiritual super-structure that every little child shall feel it to be easier to live a Christian life than an unchristian one.

You must not be in a hurry or impatient. You have not lost a man because he doesn't take the truth the first time.

Do not be discouraged because after a year you look back on your ministry and see that it is a very imperfect and wretched one, and does not answer your ambition at all. That is one of the best symptoms possible for a young man to have.

A true call to the sacred ministry is the voice of God in you speaking through your highest and noblest faculties. Any other consideration than that is not a call of God, and there are very many called, but few are chosen.

The art of putting a living heart on a living heart, that is the root of preaching.

A minister ought to be the best informed man on the face of the earth. He ought to see everything and be interested in everything.

* * *

A sermon like a probe must follow the wound into all its intricate passages. Nothing is too much for the surgeon or for the physician, nothing should be too common or too familiar for the preacher.

* * *

When you are fighting the Devil shoot him with anything.

* * *

Imagination, Emotion, Enthusiasm and Conviction, are the four foundation-stones of an effective and successful minister.

* * *

All true preaching bears the impress of the nature of the preacher.

* * *

Don't hold up any of the truths of the gospel in such a way that the man who looks at them shall say it is not possible to be sand.

* * *

Great sermons ninety-nine times in a hundred are nuisances. They are like steeples without any bells in them; things stuck up high in air, serving for ornament, attracting observation, but sheltering nobody, warming nobody, helping nobody.

A real master of men when one comes near to him, forms a judgment of the new-comer just as instinctively and as quickly as of a locomotive or a horse.

Now, when a man has a call to the ministry, he is to preach Christ and to understand Christ. He may understand a good many things out of books, he may understand a great many things out of systems, he may help himself into perplexities of experience, but, after all, the man that is the true preacher learns by the indwelling of the Holy Ghost what was the nature of that love which led Christ Jesus to empty Himself, and to go down to the bottom as it were, to the feet of the universe, that when He lifted Himself up He should carry everything with Him. It is not enough, then, that you simply have an admiration of God, and an admiration of Jesus Christ, and an approbation of Him, but you must be Christ's yourselves according to the measure of your being.

No man is fit to preach until he is fit to be sacrificed. A man that gives himself up to the work of preaching is bound to say in his ordination thought, "I will make a life-sacrifice of myself if God means it and requires it; but one thing I must do — I must be true to my own best thoughts, my own best beliefs, whether the Church likes it or not."

To preach the Gospel of Jesus Christ, to have Christ so melted and dissolved in you that when you preach your own self you preach Him as Paul did, to have every part of you living and luminous with Christ, and then to make use of everything that is in you, your analogical reasoning, your logical reasoning, your imagination, your mirthfulness, your humor, your indignation, your wrath, to take everything that is in you all steeped in Jesus Christ, and to throw yourself with all your power upon a congregation — that has been my theory of preaching the Gospel.

If a Christian man's heart is the pulpit of Christ, no sermon is needed, for there is no act of his that is not a sermon glowing with love.

The persimmon is a fruit that, while it is yet green, is bitter and puckery to the last degree, but when once it has been frosted, it is one of the sweetest of all the fruits; and there are a great many seeds — it is not until winter has dissolved in them the glue that they can open their shell and let out the root of the plumule. And there are many men that are not fit to be preachers until they have gone through the path of suffering and sorrow.

* * *

A man should introduce in his teaching something of everything that belongs to mankind; its sacred rage and passion, its abhorrence of things evil, its genius, all imagination, all the radiance and sparkle of its wit, all the tenderness of its love, all that belongs to the sub-bass, also all that belongs to the very highest stops, that seek to rival the very bird-notes. That is the greatest preacher.

* * *

A man who does not preach poor sermons will never be a good preacher. There would never be any mountains unless there were valleys between. You will never get sons of thunder in the pulpit until you get men that are willing to fail when fail they must.

* * *

Fishers of men. I should like to see fish caught by the charge of cavalry! I should like to see fastidious, hidden, sensitive fish caught by thrashing the pool with your rod or fishing line. Ye are to be fishers of men; and as men study the nature of fish — the pout, the eel nestling in the mud, the fierce pickerel, the shining trout, the gamy black bass, the salmon or the deep sea fish — and adapt their mode of fishing to the nature of the fish desired to be caught; so men are to study the mode of influence of one soul upon another, in such a way as to make the truth which they would lay before men, and into the practice of which they would draw them, efficacious and successful.

A man's truth is like bait on a hook — it must be such a bait as fish will take, and it must be on such a hook as will hold the fish.

The humblest labor which a minister of God can do for a soul for Christ's sake is grander and nobler than all learning, than all influence and power, than all riches.

If you would teach within the church, you must seek ordination at the hands of man. But whose heart soever God has touched with a spirit of benevolence is ordained to go forth into society and preach the gospel to every creature, each man speaking in the language of his own business.

Sermons that bring forth nothing in better lives are poor sermons, no matter who preaches them.

When a man pays his debts he preaches in a language that is understood by more men than when he preaches in almost any other language that is spoken.

A man should be born to the pulpit. The men that ought to preach should be ordained in birth. The laying on of hands can't make an empty head full, nor a cold heart warm, nor a silent nature vocal. A minister is a genius in moral ideas, as a poet is in beautiful ideas, and an inventor in physical ideas.

Every minister ought to turn toward every gleam of light to see if there is not some instrument by which he can better touch the hearts of men.

There is no business so derogatory that culture is not compatible with it.

There are none who stand hardship so well as those who are cultivated.

Knowledge is that which a man knows. Intelligence is that which knows it. Knowledge bears the same relation to intelligence which invested wealth does to that spirit of enterprize which creates wealth. One is the active cause. The other is the product or effect of that cause. Where knowledge will not save men, Intelligence is a preservation force.

Folk's heads are pretty much like their garrets, where all the rubbish and broken things they've no use for down-stairs are stored away.

Much of knowledge is growth, not accumulation. The life one is living in is the book that men more need to know than any other.

The first step toward knowing is to be conscious of not knowing.

If all a man's necessaries of life go in at the porthole of the stomach it is a bad sign.

The folly of the few is that light which God casts to irradiate the wisdom of the many.

Poverty is not disreputable, but Ignorance is!

In the dairy it may be all very well to have the cream on the top but it is very poor in society to have the thing repeated; for society does not move by the force of its top — that influences some — but it is the average of the mass that either accelerates or retards the movements of society in advance. It is the hull and the freight, and not the sails alone, that determine the quickness of the voyage, and ignorance at the bottom of society benumbs society; it is obliged to drag this vast bulk. It is like a gouty man trying to walk; he may be good at the top and all the way down, but his feet are not good, and he cannot walk. There can be no prosperity that is deserving of that name that leaves at the bottom a section of ignorance nearly equal to that in the middle or top of society.

All property is matter that has been shaped to uses by intelligent skill. Where intelligence is low, the power of producing property is low. It is the husbandman who thinks, foresees, plans, and calls on all natural laws to serve him, whose farm brings forth forty, fifty and a hundred fold. The ignorant peasant grubs and groans and reaps but one handful where he has sown two. It is knowledge that is the gold mine, for although every knowing man may not be able to be a rich man, out of ignorance riches do not spring anywhere.

Ignorant men are like bombs, which are a great deal better to be shot into an enemy's camp than to be kept at home, for where an ignorant man goes off he scatters desolation, and it is not safe to have ignorant men.

Ignorance enslaves men among men, knowledge is the factor and the great creator of liberty and wealth.

Ignorance is the fruitful mother of mischief.

Hope is an anchor that holds on to the bottom while the storms handle the ship, and enables it to outride the tempest.

* *

Hope doesn't believe in sunset, nor in the rolling hours that bring round again the sunrise; it is forever facing toward the east and waiting for the sun to rise. It is the power to live without bodily organization; it is that element of the spirit that sees all that is unrevealed by matter; it is that temper that lives in the glowing future and in the possibilities of blossom and fruit, of an eternal summer that lies before every man, that does not live in yesterday, that refuses to live in to-day, but that takes the eternal round of the future for its habitation.

* *

Hope is the sweet eye that never looks backward, the disposition that eternally lives on, which cures present evil, remedies every mistake, by an eternal sunrise.

* *

In the ministration of God's Providence in this world, tears and heartbreak, and all forms of moral or social suffering are good for what they do to a man who is sick or out of the way, but when he is brought by suffering into some affinity with the right way, suffering is not the type of the right way, but joy, peace, hope. We are saved by hope; we are saved by the finer instincts and finer influences of the human soul; not by the dread, the captivity, the bondage, the crutch, the odious medicine.

⁂

Do I believe in election! I certainly do. I believe that some men are elected to be mathematicians, and some I know are not. I believe some men are elected to be poets; some are not. Some men are elected to think with the perceptive faculties, and some are left out of that election. Some are elected to be thoughtful with the philosophical faculties, and others are not so elected. Now there are a great many men who are "elected". That is, they are born of their mother and father with such moral susceptibilities that they can take in the idea of this soul-filling, soul-enriching and soul-rejoicing God. There are others that are born so that they can take it in but imperfectly, little by little, and only as the result of long continued education. This is election — receptive capacity. It is inside election, not outside election.

⁂

When a man emerges through the gate of death into the other land he is not perfect. No miracle is wrought on him. He goes from the primary school to the university. There is to be a wide sphere, and a long period — we know not how long — in which all these relatively developed or cruder elements of humanity will undergo in the next and higher sphere the working of the Spirit of God through Jesus Christ.

* * *

Some men think that they are converted because they had a horrible conviction, and because they said they were brought out of the miry clay, and had their feet set upon the rock. They look back to that experience and they say, "I was converted at four o'clock in the afternoon on the tenth of June, eighteen hundred and so and so." Your clock may be right, but the thing itself is not perhaps worthy of a revelation; for I have not been able to perceive that you are a particle less proud; I think on some grounds you are more avaricious; I think you have traded on your reputation for piety; I think you have taken on airs by reason of your supposed now superiority. When a man is converted he says, "I saw a great light". It was nothing but a tallow candle, and the wind blew it out very soon. Yet the man carries round his snuffed-out candle and says, "I was converted". Some men who are converted carry about their lamps which are known by the smoking of the unburnt material, and they think that they have got a light. They do not bring forth the fruit of love.

The very first intimation that any man has of a conviction is when he begins to say to himself, "I am not living right".

If you want conviction of sin, try to live as you know you ought to live. If that does not convict you of sin I do not know what will.

To him that is born to sing, singing is a necessity; and to him that is born to sigh, sighing is a necessity. Some smile easily, and some are just as easily sad. Some think. Some feel. Each has his mood.

A grumbling man might have a band of angels to pilot him around about the globe, and he could not find happiness.

God loves cheerfulness and mirth, or he would not have sunk the fountains of them so deep in the best parts of the human soul.

How useless are all frets and cares and bickerings, not only, but how much pain they bring; how they rasp life until its tender places are enameled, hardened with a mean and vulgar face. How inconsistent to be fretting, morose, fearing, dreading, trembling, and yet in our hymns and in our devotions to be calling ourselves the sons of God! We wallow, and then sing that we are born again as heirs of eternal glory! If there be anything in this world that ought to mark a Christian man, it is not tears, not sorrow, not wailing, but joy in the Holy Ghost. Hope, trust, love — these are the Trinity. Now abideth faith, hope, love; and the greatest of these is love; but they are all indispensable. In these triune stars, this trinity of qualities, living in a world that is God's, under a providence and a spiritual ministration that is God's, in the hope of God and the certainty of immortality in Him, life ought to wear a smile, and sorrow itself to be a benediction. That man who misinterprets Christianity by going morosely and sadly through life ought to apologize to every person to whom he comes, for his habiliment of sorrow, and for the mistranslation of God's government over him.

Two acres of wilderness adjoining—that is married life with multitudes of people. But where two strive together, not each for his or her own excellence, where the soul of each would throw its light over for illumination upon the other soul, how sacred is wedlock!

No man is married by his body to his wife, any more than two slaves are married that are linked together to go across the desert to their prison-house. All true marriage is inside. Men may be held and should be, by the law, to the fidelities of even the most exterior relationship in marriage; wedlock is sacred even at its very lowest contact; but oh, how many steps onward and upward does the marriage relation contain in itself! They are married that are agreeable in person to each other; they are married that intersphere in intelligence with each other; they are married that have reciprocal tastes; they are married that have love purities within the sphere of their crystalline beings; they are married that are heroic together; and they are married that together aspire to live larger and better lives.

Men have a little boat of piety which runs up and down the waves of their experience; but their life is a great hull of selfishness, the bow of which is rigged with the lower passions.

Indifference to men is a sin. It is not necessary to your being a criminal that you should murder, or commit burglary, or set a house on fire, or pick some man's pocket. If you take your culture, and taste, and sensibility, and wrap yourself up in them, and walk alone among your fellowmen, touching nobody, kindling nobody, sympathizing with nobody, except one here and there whom you select as a companion for yourself, you are criminal before God; and there is many a man who walks thus who is a greater sinner than the man who is hanged, for the law of Christian sympathy is absolute; it is the imperial law of the realm. It is the ideal of Christian life; and he who violates it by counting his fellowmen as nothing, as dust under his feet, as dirt, violates the fundamental law of the universe, and is a criminal.

* * *

If there is one thing that stood out more strongly than any other in the ministry of our Lord it is the severity with which he treated the exclusiveness of men with knowledge, position, and a certain sort of religion, a religion of particularity and carefulness; if there is one class of the community against which he hurled his thunderbolts without mercy and predicted woes, it was the scribes, Pharisees, scholars and priests of the temples. He told them in so many words, "The publican and the harlot will enter the kingdom of God before you". The worst dissipation in this world is the dry-rot of morality and of the so-called piety that separates men of prosperity and of power from the poor and ignoble. They are our wards. When God looks out of heaven, He looks at the bottom of things first and at the top last; and therefore he says, "He that will be chief among you, let him become your slave". He that would stand highest, let him be the man who has gone down to the very foundation of human life and society, in order to lift men up. As God gave himself for the salvation of the world, so the follower of Christ is to give his life-power for the salvation of the inferior and the lowest throughout the whole world.

Where the human soul acts inwardly, making all creation run in upon it, to fan it, to flatter it, to please it, to enrich it, the machinery is wound up the wrong way. It is not thus that the soul is made to be harmonious or happy. When a man's nature acts centrifugally, going forth in the spirit of kindness and benevolence, he is happy. It is what a man does for others that constitutes true happiness — not what he does for himself.

***

The dissipation of the top of the brain is worse than the dissipation of the bottom of the brain. A man who uses his knowledge and his moral training to increase his selfishness and his contempt of his fellowmen is worse than the man who abuses his natural passions and corrupts them.

***

How easy to be patient when we are sure that patience is victory! Wait, and die, and see, and be happy.

***

When I think how we, in all our crooked ways of deceit and dissimulation must appear to the peerless honor, the sensitive holiness and purity of the soul of

God; patience seems the most stupendous of His attributes.

* * *

If we find pain in the effort to do and to be right it is through the imperfection of our attainment. Perfect consecration always brings peace and joy.

* * *

There is a peace that comes by quickening the tone of a man's nerves. It is not the peace of somnolency; it is that perfect rest which the soul has when it is in all its members satisfied — filled full of that for which it hungers and thirsts. It is the rest of impletion. That is the testimony of ten thousand saints who have lived since the advent of Christ. It is peace not only in the ordinary avocations of life, but in all the exigencies that try men's souls. There has never been a dying saint that had profounder rest and peace in God than men have had who were fastened to the stake with fagots tied around their bodies, so great is the power of God upon the inward life.

* * *

It is high up that the most perfect peace is. There are places in the nooks and ravines of the mountains where there is peace; but they who go up in balloons say that as they rise above the earth all sounds die away, and that high up in the pure ether there is perfect silence. And so, as men rise through the experience and trials of life, they find that high up there is a realm of peace.

* * *

The method of Christ's teaching was not philosophical, nor was it logical. In part it was pictorial, dramatic; but mostly it was annunciatory. He made simple statements, leaving them to their own force, and to the realization through experience of those that accepted them. It was as if there was in human thought and language neither any approach nor any form of argument. They were facts so high, so profound, that they could be only announced — not fortified by speech. No other teacher that ever appeared had the imperial love that Christ had, or so made Himself, His own system, the substance of His doctrine. It was not, "Come to Me, and I will show you the way to God". It was, "Come unto Me, and I will give you rest". He was a door through which men were to come into the kingdom. He was a vine, and they were to be His branches. He declared that outside of Him, or without Him, they could do nothing. Everywhere He assumed in Himself the whole theory, philosophy and substance of His teaching.

* * *

Christ taught by fiction. His parables are pictures addressed to the imagination; and they produce in the minds of men more correct impressions of the truth than any mere statement of fact could produce. There is a constant play in Christ's teaching between light and dark, between knowing and not knowing, between the infinite and the limited.

Now, if Christ was only a great man, we should not expect that there would be this play in His teaching. You do not see it in the writings of Goethe or of Shakespeare except when they are describing it in others as the fruit and product of inspiration. If the Lord Jesus Christ had squared and jointed everything by rule and law it might have been said, "There is one who works like a man in the limitations of the earthly sphere". But He does not; He acts as one who is subject to limitation, and recognizes it; He has mystery above Him, and speaks truths that are out of our reach; He gives evidence in His appearance, in His conversation and in His discourses, of one who is familiar with the upper, spiritual and invisible sphere, and Who is attempting, by His life and teaching, to interpret it in the lower, physical and visible sphere. So there is in the life of Christ a manifestation of divinity; a double consciousness; a sense of things in this world, and a sense of things infinitely beyond this world, with thoughts and feelings playing back and forth between heaven and earth, like a shuttle in a loom carrying a golden thread, the upper part of the fabric being invisible, and only the lower part, where it touches him, being visible.

Advice to unwilling men is like hail-stones on slate

roofs; it strikes and rattles and rolls down and does them no good.

* * *

It's surprisin' how we take advice that travels the same way we do! It's like hittin' a ball the same way it's rollin' a'ready.

* * *

Love of beauty is not love of God, but if through this outer court of the temple you come more easily into His presence, go by that way. The child has a right to nestle in his father's bosom, by whatever means he has climbed to it.

* * *

Intelligence implies a certain condition of the knowing faculties. Knowledge is the fruit of intelligence. There is just as much difference between them as there is between skill and the product of skill, or between husbandry and the harvests that husbandry can produce. A man may have intelligence and scarcely any knowledge. A man may have a good deal of knowledge and hardly any intelligence. We see men that have plunged right and left into history in all directions, but that are not intelligent after all. They are cumbered by their knowledge; they do not know what to do with it; and they are no more rich in knowledge than the ass that carries gold from the mine to the mint is rich in gold. But where one has both intelligence and knowledge and is growing in them both, that is a transcendently noble thing.

* * *

Hate a lie! A liar is worse than the man who has got the plague. You cannot afford to be liars; and you connot afford to be truth speakers unless you live worthy of the truth.

* * *

It is not necessary that a man should always tell everything, but whatever he tells, it is necessary that that should always be truth.

* * *

A man has a right to concealment. The soul has no more business to go stark naked down the street than a man has to go stark naked as regards his body. A man that has not a great silence in him, a great reserve in him, is not half a man — he is a babbler, he leaks at the mouth.

* * *

If lying were more common than speaking the truth, society would be like a heap of sand, it would fall apart. The cohesion is the belief in men's veracity. A lie has to have a cutting edge of truth or it would not be worth anything. It is the truth that works a lie into anything like victory.

* * *

A man that will not tell the truth without an oath won't tell the truth with an oath. You cannot make a man honest by machinery. There has got to be established in him an automatic honesty, an honesty individual.

* * *

There are different sizes of feathers on an eagle; there are wing-feathers, and tail-feathers, and down. And there are wing-feather lies, and tail-feather lies, and downy lies. You can lie without opening your mouth, as well as by opening it. Your little finger can lie as well as your tongue.

* * *

I think we must judge of human character as men do of timber. I do not care what a man's character may be, the effect upon it of his telling a lie is what a worm channel is in a sill of oak. When a stick of timber has one worm channel running through it, it may be a strong stick of timber yet, but it is weakened some. When it comes to have two or three of these channels running through it, it is good for nothing.

* *

Oh, dear! Shall we ever get done with lying? It is one of the few domestic manufactures which need no protection, and flourish without benefit to the producer or consumer.

* *

I believe there are folks who do not lie in thought or in feeling; but they are all in heaven. On earth, when a man so lives that everybody can see him inside and out, from his perfect truthfulness — when a man speaks the truth absolutely he has got to be a man so good that the Lord does not keep him here long. I do not speak of vulgar bluntness, but I speak of that state of mind in which the love of truth in the very inward parts prevails and dominates the life; the yea is yea, and the nay is nay, and there is no shading off of either of them.

* *

A broken-down scholar is like a razor without a handle. The finest edge on the best steel is beholden to the services of homely horn for ability to be useful. Never out-run health.

* *

I have reason to believe that a good deal of the theology of the past has sprung from dyspepsia; that a great deal of the tormenting aspects that have been given to the sweetness of Divine truth has arisen from the melancholia of men that have lost digestion, or who have enthroned the blue devils in their liver. Health is morality to a large extent — the foundation of it anyhow.

* * *

The foundation of real activity, and the foundation of normal conditions of disposition, lies in good, substantial sound health

* * *

A man without any constitution is like a cannon with a cornstalk carriage under it, and every time he fires it off he knocks the carriage over, and by and by destroys it.

* * *

To grow up in good sound health, without violation of the great canons of morality, and with the law of moderation fixed upon every appetite and passion, is no insignificant ideal for a young man or woman.

* * *

A man who spends his whole force to save his soul, has not much of a soul, nor one that is worth saving. It is the quintessence of selfishness.

* * *

No man can live to the flesh, and reap life everlasting. Be not deceived; God is not easily mocked, and no man can live here to selfishness, passion, appetite, self-seeking, lust, and all the under corrosive appetite and reap life everlasting.

When a man goes out of life he sinks from sight like the extinguished taper, if he has lived in the animal exclusively; but if there has been in him a seed worth planting again, I believe he will be planted under a fairer sky and in a better soil, and with ten thousand temptations removed from him which are incident to this life, and that we shall see through the circling ages many redeemed after life, cleansed from the body and from selfishness, and educated into higher spiritual aspiration, and into the great love-knowledge of God's universe. Those that live in this life achieving victory, and that know how to speak the language of heaven shall be caught up without anything intermediate, and be with the Lord at once.

When I think about the condition of men after death, I think of all Africa, and that, too, for thousands of years; I think of all Asia, and that for myriads of years; of every island of the sea; of the population that is for multitude more than the drops of water in the ocean forty times magnified; of that vast sweep of creation, illimitable, uncountable, of human beings that have been created in conditions that imply and necessitate imperfection, and ask myself, "What has God done for them all? Where are they? Are they wailing in immitigable torment?" If that be so, never let me mention the name of God again. Let me never violate my own nature by calling him "Father". Such dogma applied to the race through all past time derides, despises, and treads under foot the very foundation ideas which we have of fatherhood.

* * *

What has annihilation in it so terrible as the continued existence of unfit natures? What happens when the taper goes out? The earth does not shake. The sun does not stop. Nobody notices it. It simply goes out. And when a man has spent the forces of life here, and has not reached the condition which makes another stage possible to him, suppose he simply goes out? What inhumanity is that, or what shock? He that would live on must live well now; and if he does not begin in his future conditions at the highest point conceivable, he may live high enough up to take a new road and a new start, under better and more favorable circumstances, justifying the wisdom of his having been "subjected in hope" to this existence of change and struggle; and in the endless ages of growth, by the "abiding" forces of faith and hope and love, he "shall be delivered from the bondage of corruption into the glorious liberty of the children of God". But as for those that go persistently and steadily lower and lower until they lose the susceptibility and the possibility of human evolution and moral development, suppose the end of the body is the end of life for them? In the great abyss of nothingness there is no groan, no sorrow, no pain, no memory! It is the theory of endless conscious misery of imperfection and wickedness without hope, that accuses the Father Creator of cruelty.

Envying is covetousness, or worse; it is the recognition of good fortune, or of attainment, or of power, or of something else in those that are above, and the man is angry at their goodness because it rebukes his meanness or his littleness.

What if they are better and more popular than you? Thank God that there is some one better and more popular than you. What if they are wiser than you? Thank God that there is one more star in the firmament above yourself. What if they have the commendation of men while you have only the dry bitter root to chew? Thank God that somewhere there is somebody that is not getting troubled as you are. There are tears enough, and misfortunes enough, and there are burdens and cares laid on those that are eminent quite enough to keep them down in their own estate.

"It is a rare friendship that will tell a man his

faults. A man will take almost anything else in hand sooner than he will offend a friend by saying to him, 'You are liable, here, to downfall and disgrace'; and before a man knows his failings himself everybody else knows them."

* * *

Friends dwelling together in the most perfect unity and sympathy hardly need to talk. The action interprets itself, a look interprets itself, and it is almost the beginning of that spiritual experience of the other life yet to come by which, doubtless, we shall know as we are known without communication, by which we shall see, by which we shall hear, without eye and without ear; the power of the spirit to translate itself into another spirit, without the instruments and the narrow media that belong to our earthly life. And that power which we have on earth developed very slenderly, may also be developed in our relationship with God, so that we may say every day, "I am His, and He is mine, what can I wish for more?"

Looking at persons from the critical point of view is almost fatal to friendship. Criticism of the faults of friends is consistent if you have a very large disposition of charity. You do not need to blind yourself to weaknesses; but no man is fit for friendship who has not the love that overcomes faults in those whom he loves. You must not make friends of those who are so different from you, so far removed from your habits of mind, as that you cannot encompass them with your charity and love.

* * *

If you cut off a branch of a tree, and immediately bandage it, so as not to allow the air to get at the wound, it will grow again; but if you crack a crystal vase, no growing process in creation will repair the damage. It is cracked glass forever and forever. Nothing will take out the crack. Now, although a cracked friendship, like a cracked tumbler, may be cemented, the moment you put it into hot water the bottom will fall out, or it will come to pieces.

* * *

Christ went forth bearing his cross — not dragging it. And we are to bear our crosses. We are to bear them in such a way that men, looking upon us, shall have something to admire and something to imitate.

There are many persons who, having their cross put upon them, and not being at liberty to choose whether they will bear it or not, drag it upon the ground. How many persons there are that go groaning and grumbling and repining, because they cannot get away from certain things! I never feel the south wind, that I do not smell flowers, I never feel the northeast wind that I do not smell storms. There are some who are gardenesque to me, and there are others who remind me of winds that blow across New Foundland, and bring fogs, dreary and dismal. They live in a perpetual cold sizzle of disappointment, disagreeable and complaining. Oh no! They do not mean to give up; they will not lay aside their cross; but alas! they are bearing that hated cross right through the mud along the thoroughfare. The cross is a clog to them.

Every true cross-bearer learns to carry his cross as if it was an ornament, rather than a burden, and finds, after a time, that it carries him. It gives more strength to him than he gives to it.

I marvel that there are not more victories. I marvel that there is not more glorying over the cross. I marvel that there are not more songs of victory sung. For there is no joy greater than that of grief overcome. Nothing is more joyous in this world than the song of one who has risen from a lower to a higher plane.

It is said that an unhelped cross is the heaviest thing a man ever carried; but a Christ-touched cross is about the lightest thing a man ever carried.

When God breaks up your plans, and throws you to the very ground, and breaks all the threads in the loom which you were weaving, and says to you, "Begin again", is there any Christ for you at that point of overthrow? Can you go forth unto your Saviour marking that place in his life where he was overthrown, identifying it in some way by association with your overthrow? Can you stand rejoicing with Christ at that very point of humiliation and crucifixion? How noble are the opportunities! How seldom are men, themselves, noble enough to know their opportunities! And the best things to polish us, the best things to strengthen us, the best influences to bring us near to Christ, we go mourning over, as if they were the graveyards of our hope. They are not; they are open windows of God through which shines the bright light of the higher life.

What care I where I am if I am only where Christ put me! A faithful soldier, who knows that the general's eye is upon him, cares not whether he is detailed for this duty or for that. It is a matter of indifference to him whether he is placed at a point of peril or a point of safety. His desire is to serve his leader as best he can. A man will fulfill the commands of one whom he esteems, reveres, worships; and when a man is Christ's and realizes it, he trusts him implicitly.

The man who trusts in God, lives in the upper story of his head; while the man who does not trust in God, lives in the lower story of his head. The man who trusts in God, lives in an observatory, where he enjoys the sunlight and the pure atmosphere of heaven; while the man who does not trust in God, lives down in a dark and dungeon cellar.

***

Let the world rock. If the foot of God is on the cradle, fear not.

***

Throw away that misleading word "unity". Put in its place instead the word "harmony", and then all theology will be reconciled and reconcilable. Then we can go all together though we differ, yea, the more can we rejoice going together that we differ. The infantry need never envy the cavalry nor the artillery the infantry. They are all composite elements of the one grand army, and each helps in its place to bring about the victory; and when the victory is attained there are no diversities and no disputes about the harmonized elements.

***

Harmony is not a monotone. Harmony is not unison. It is concordant differences.

***

God is forever producing difference. Men, stupidly, are forever striving to rub it out. God never allows anything to go through two generations just alike, and we are coopering up the work of God, or trying to do it, and to restore a certain sort of lost unity or identity.

* * *

That is not the true church which is largest, or the most numerous, or the most decorated, or the most acerb in its theology, or the most historic in its claims; but that which continually brings forth the sweet fruits of righteousness in the form of love.

* * *

The only unity this world will ever see, or that God wants it to see, is unity of spirit, unity of love, of sympathy, of helpfulness.

* * *

The sense, the physical body, is the instrument by which the world acts upon our hidden man, and by which the hidden man acts back again upon the world. It is as with an organ. What is there in the pressure that is given by the hand, and what is there in the wild winds that are confined in the bellows, that should be converted into aerial music, stirring up every passion, every admiration, every joy and pleasure in the human soul? The man gives impulse by touch and by mechanical aids, and the moment the organ receives that, it responds and rolls out those grand anthems that have filled the arches of cathedrals and the arch of Time itself. That which the instrument is, man is; more wonderfully, more variously, more beautifully, receiving touch from all nature and the diffused God in it; and then as a son of God, giving back in different forms and in different melodies and harmonies, the impulse and the results.

A pocket is like a cistern, a small leak at the bottom is more than a large pump at the top. God sends rain enough every year, but it is not every man that will take pains to catch it, and it is not every man who catches it who knows how to keep it.

The great trouble with men is not a lack of opportunity, it is the need of disposition to improve the opportunities they have. Our trouble is not to know what to do, it is to have a heart to do what we know.

Some of the best things that men ever do are things that they do as it were, accidentally. The best things that a man says are not the things he sets out to say, but those that he says without thinking. A whole lifetime is sometimes crowded into a single moment.

He only who made the heart can touch all the chords.

* *

Home should be an oratorio of the memory, singing to all one's after life melodies and harmonies of old-remembered joy.

* *

Conceit is narrow. No man can be very broad who will build with nothing but that which he quarries from himself. There are men enough who think when they hear themselves echoed, that a God spoke.

* *

The whole spirit of the New Testament is in favor of the resurrection in a form which shall answer to our earthly body, and that, in some high and noble way, belongs to it. As the blossom to the bud, as the flower to the seed. In that sacred hope we cherish the body, and bury it as one might bury a tulip, hyacinth, or narcissus — a homely bulb — but how beautiful the flower, when all-resurrecting spring shall call for it, and the answer shall be a fragrant blossom.

* *

Taste in its time and proportion, is one element of religion.

Matter-of-fact things are good; but they are infinitely better where they are accompanied by taste and reason and veneration and beneficence, than where they are without these accompaniments; for the whole is better than any single element.

* * *

Three elements enter into the creed of a great citizen. That which his ancestry gives. That which opportunity gives. That which his will developes.

* * *

The spark that was kindled at Fort Sumter fell upon the North like fire upon Autumnal prairies. Men came together in the presence of this universal calamity with sudden fusion. They forgot all separations of politics, parties or even religion itself. It was a conflagration of patriotism. The bugle and the drum rung out in every neighborhood; the plough stood still in the furrow; the hammer dropped from the anvil; work and pen were forgotten; pulpit and forum, court and shop felt the electric shock. Parties dissolved and re-formed. The Democratic party sent forth a host of noble men and swelled the Republican ranks, and gave many noble leaders and irresistible energy to the hosts of War. The whole land became a military school, and officers and men began to learn the art and practice of war.

* * *

The South had builded herself upon the rock of Slavery. It lay in the very channels of Civilization like some Flood Rock lying sullen off Hell Gate. The tides of controversy rushed upon it, and split into eddies and swirling pools, bringing incessant disaster. The rock would not move. It must be removed. It was the South itself that furnished the engineers. Arrogance in Council sunk the shaft, Violence clanked the subterranean passages, and Infatuation loaded them with infernal dynamite. All was secure. Their rock was their fortress. The hand that fired Sumter exploded the mine, and tore the fortress to atoms. For one moment it rose into the air like spectral hills; for one moment the water rocked with wild confusion, then settled back to quiet and the way of Civilization was opened!

* * *

As Christ has embraced the human soul in his own, so hath he taught me to call all men my brethren.

* * *

It is very easy for a man to hate evil and not love good. The two things come from two different sides of the brain. A man hates error with the bottom of his brain. He loves truth with the top of his brain.

* * *

I am for war just so far as it is necessary to vindicate a great moral truth. But one particle of violence beyond that is a flagrant treason against the law of love. I would go to war with every state in the Southern Confederacy, if called to go into the army, and would hold them to the conflict till the cause of right was vindicated; and then I could at the same time pray for those misguided men, as easily as to-night I can pray for my babes. I regard them as citizens yet, I love this whole country. I love it in its past and in its prospective history. God do so to me, and more also, if that hour comes when I do not feel for them, misguided though they be, as anxiously as for my own kin and brethren.

* * *

On Sunday morning, the fourteenth of April, it was known that Sumter had surrendered. The scales fell from men's eyes!

There was war!

The flag of the Nation had been pierced by men who had been taught their fatal skill under its protection! The Nation's pride, its love, its honor suffered with that flag, and with it trailed in humiliation.

Without concert, or council, the whole people rose suddenly with one indignation to vindicate the Nation's honor. It came as the night comes, or the morning — broad as a hemisphere. It rose as the tides raise the whole ocean, along the whole continent, drawn upward by the whole heavens.

* * *

Some days seem to be characterized by some single sense. There are head-days and heart-days, and there are eye-days and ear-days and promiscuous days, in which delicious sensations of pleasure at life in general predominate. These last are transcendent.
We are filled with the very affluence of peacefulness and joy. There is neither sorrow nor want nor madness nor trouble, in the wide world! But such days have no art to perpetuate themselves. To-morrow will sweep you to the opposite pole. Yet they are of great use. They exalt our ideal of life. Subjects held up in their light will never be as low and ignoble as they may have been before. And the light in which Duty, Love and Labor, shine in these lucid days will give us exaltation for many days after.

* * *

Flowers have an expression of countenance as much as men or animals. Some seem to smile; some have a sad expression; some are pensive and diffident; others again are plain, honest and upright, like the broad-faced sunflower and hollyhock. What a pity flowers can utter no sound! A singing rose, a whispering violet, a murmuring honeysuckle! Oh, what a rare and exquisite miracle would these be.

* * *

I love a flower that all may have; that belongs to the whole, and not to a select and exclusive few. Common, forsooth! A flower cannot be worn out by much looking at, as a road is by much travel.

* * *

It is a shame for a generation to die bankrupt. Every generation should take what has been already gained as capital, and die richer than it was born, leaving an inheritance of noble ideas to its successors.

* * *

The newspaper is the carrier of preaching. When a man is conscious that what he is saying to-day in the air will be proclaimed on the housetop by the outrunning newspapers, he cannot but have larger thought, and a larger sympathy, and a larger influence.

* * *

Newspapers are the schoolmasters of the common people.

* * *

A man who can only work and not think, is not the equal in any regard of the man who can think, who can plan, who can combine, and who can live not for to-day alone but for to-morrow, for next month, for the next year, for ten years. This is the man whose volume will just as surely weigh down that of the unthinking man, as a ton will weigh down a pound in the scale. Avoirdupois is moral, industrial, as well as material, in this respect; and the primary cause therefore of unprosperity in industrial callings lies in the want of intelligence, either in the slender endowment of the man, or, more likely, the want of education in his ordinary and average endowment.

A man is not to be educated because an education will help him to thrift in life, but because he is a man. It is his business to make his manhood larger; and education means manhood, all sidedness, in men.

I think the days that precede millennial glory will have some other way than rote teaching, or the mere stuffing of a child with knowledge in some departments, leaving life really to be his great educator; for when a man goes out now into life too sensitive, he very soon is ready, in the shop or in his profession, to repress the sensibility that he has in over measure; or he is too blunt and loses customers until he begins to smile and become courteous; he learns it behind the counter, this looking upon everybody as if they were unlike everybody else, until by diversity of experience he finds out how different men are. The road to the front door of a man lies in a very different direction, in different individuals. Some men have got no door but a back door, and some men have got a side door, and some a front door. Some men have got only a scuttle in the roof; you have to go down that to get into them; and there is no instruction provided for in our courses, in our schools, on these fundamental differences among mankind. Men are left to pick them up; the stupid never do, and the bright do, and use them to their own advantage, selfishly. Do you suppose the human race is to go on forever and forever in that way, and a man's internal structure be an enigma, and the method of training it lag far behind the training that the athlete gives to the bodily organs? No; the day will come when men will understand the inside just as well as the outside.

There are a great many fathers and mothers whose nature is to govern. The spirit of autocracy and monarchy is in them. They do not govern their children to teach those children to govern themselves, but they govern them for the sake of governing them; and they keep it up; and the children never learn self-government.

The object of governing a child is to get rid of the necessity of governing him. It is to teach him the use of his own faculties with regard to the great laws which are fundamental to you and him in common.

If you bring up your children with a liberty which has restriction enough to make them obey the law, and with an amount of government which make them independent and self-reliant, you will do that which is best for them. They will make blunders; but they will learn. They will fall into mistakes; but those mistakes will be part of their training. You can bring up a child so that he is all compliance toward externality; but he will have no power in himself; and will never amount to anything. These round, smooth folks, that come up so carefully, and that will roll all ways with equal facility, and are of no particular account, serving as mere punctuation points to keep other folks apart, have not been well developed, or taught, or bred.

Communities and nations are to be developed by the development of men, and not by the enactments of legislation. Legislation may do some things; it may remove some obstacles; it may facilitate progress; but after all, the indispensable condition by which the great mass of working men, at home and abroad, are to acquire place, and ease, and comfort, is that they shall be trained and cultured.

He that would go up must go up by the elevation of his being. It is being which makes rank and condition, substantially.

The invisible — how rich it is! How mightier than

the visible! Visible things are mixed, confused, uncertain and unreliable; but in the invisible and moral, measures are never jarred; they are always right; and there is a place where the sigh is louder than the trumpet of praise among men.

The invisible things in this world are more wonderful than the visible. It is not the things that address themselves to our eyes, or to our ears, or to our hands, that are the most wonderful, even in nature. The silent elements, the unseen forces, the chemists in the roots, the mighty monarchs of power hidden in clouds, the energies of nature, the products which we see, but not the causes — these are streaming forth evermore; but we are too coarsely made to appreciate them, and we only see the outcome — not the work of exquisite elements that are producing the results of nature. If the soul could only have its outcome and product rendered visible, still more marvelous would be the exhalation, as it were, of life that would ascend and fill the whole air. If all the emotions that rise in every soul through one single live-long day could address themselves either to the eye or to the ear, how many dramas that are never written would there be!

How many concerts that are never heard would play in the air! What hope, what fear, what sorrow, what joy, what tenderness of love, what rudeness of anger, what despotism of pride, what throngs of ever-weaving fancies, what strange thoughts of things, or qualities of imagination, what faith, what enormous productiveness there is in the silence of every human soul, and the unwritten realities of human life put to shame, whether in fearfulness or in grandeur, all that literature ever indited! We lose, we waste the most precious part; and human life, like an unstopped vase of effervescent and perishing quality, exhales and throws off into the absolute and the eternal the very best portions of itself. The detritus, and often only that, remains.

Whatever there is of purity, of hope, of generous sentiment, of courage, of magnanimity or of fidelity, never dies. As the sun draws invisible particles from the river and the sea, and holds them in the air, cloud-treasures from which the earth supplies itself, so each generation finds itself compassed about with this "great cloud of witnesses", that rain down moral influence upon generation after generation. All that men call real, practical and substantial, is the most perishable. That which men call imaginary, impracticable and theoretic often lives forever.

How society teaches us to wash the outside of the

cup, or the platter, or the dish! How much there is infamous before God and stenchful before men, if it were only brought out and made known to us. This hidden man is more beautiful than any of you think, and more horrible. The saint dwells in many a bosom, not far removed from the very angels of the throne itself. Devils inhabit the heart of many and many a "respectable" man. O, bring out your silent man; make him speak, unroll what is written in his thought. Bring from the loom of his inward activity the fabric, and let men see what he has wrought, and what figures are worked into the pattern. How many men could hold up their faces then? And how many men who have produced nothing for the market, not much for the neighborhood, little for the uses that are common on earth; that have neither the pen of the ready writer, nor the tongue of the orator, nor the wings of the poet, are rich unto God? They dwelt in their meditations, and their imaginations remain untranslated into human language or into human conditions, but they are rich toward God.

A man is what he thinks, a man is what he feels, a man is what he desires. In other words, the hidden man is the real man that goes to judgment; not what we work out but what we desire to work out; not merely the moral character of the act that is completed but he moral character of the intention and design within.

The moment a man begins to think about dishonesty he has half committed it; the moment a man begins to think about a lie he has half told it.

There is succor for every man who is tempted, no matter how low he may be. There are men who stand in the shadow of perdition; there are men who, from the very beginning, count themselves unworthy of hope; and yet no temptation befalls a man that is so low, or so gross, or so brutal, that he cannot carry it into the presence of Christ, and say, "Oh, thou Tempted in All Points as I Am, help me", for that is His name — Tempted in All Points as I Am.

There are many men who are like an apple-tree in my garden, whose trunk and roots, and two-thirds of the branches, are in the garden, and one-third of whose branches are outside the garden-wall. And there are many men whose trunk and roots are on the side of honesty and uprightness, but who are living so near the garden-wall that they throw their boughs clear over into the highway where iniquities tramp, and are free.

It is never safe for a man to run so near to the line of right and wrong, that if he should lose a wheel he would go over. It is like traveling on a mountain road near a precipice. You should keep so far from the precipice that if your wagon breaks down there is room enough between you and the precipice.

* * *

There are some things that it is a sin to look at twice. And yet there are men who hunt them up.

* * *

I do not believe in bringing up the young to know life, as it is said. I should just as soon think of bringing up a child by cutting some of the cords of his body and lacerating his nerves and scarring and tattooing him, and making an Indian of him outright, as an element of beauty, as I should think of developing his manhood by bringing him up to see life — to see its abominable lusts, to see its hideous incarnations of wit, to see its infernal wickedness, to see its extravagant and degrading scenes, to see its miserable carnalities, to see its imaginations set on fire of hell, to see all those temptations and delusions which lead to perdition. Nobody gets over the sight of these things. They who see them always carry scars. They are burned. And though they live, they live as men that have been burned. The scar remains.

* * *

It is dangerous for men to indulge in pleasures

which stand near temptations. It is dangerous for men to stand in the neighborhood of such temptations. I do not care how innocent the things are *per se*. It was perfectly innocent for me to ride a mule up the sides of Swiss mountains, but it was perfectly provoking the way the mule would take the very edge of the path, when there was a precipice three or four thousand feet deep below me, so that if the animal had made a misstep I would have been dashed to pieces. Thousands of men are riding mules — that is, themselves — on the outer edge of dangerous paths; and it will only require one small mistake to throw them to the bottom of a deep precipice. And no man has a right to live even a moral life, in such a way that his path winds around so near a precipice that the slightest deviation from the exact course shall destroy him.

A man may act from strong selfish motives, and from strong avaricious motives, and yet there may be mingled with these higher motives. This question then comes up, when there are mixed motives: "Does the presence of the lower vitiate or destroy the higher!" No. It adulterates it, but it does not destroy it. Where a man acts for a right thing from a pure motive; where a man sees the truth and follows it conscientiously, from love to God, from love to man, and from love to the truth itself, that is the highest form of conduct. But if afterwards there is the consciousness in his bosom that while he acts from these higher motives interest comes in, this lower motive does not vitiate the others. It is his duty to see that the lower motive is kept in its proper place, but the higher motives are not destroyed by the existence of the lower one. A man is not necessarily a hypocrite who acts from different classes of motives; but he who acts from a lower class of motives under the pretense that he is acting from a higher class, is hypocritical.

There is nothimg more common than for men to hang one motive outside where it can be seen, and keep the other in the background to turn the machinery.

God destroys only that he may multiply. A great nature springs up, and the world seems to pivot on him; and men, when they hear of his decease, hold up their hands in panic, and say, "All the strings of affairs were tied to him, and now they are broken loose". If a man is a great man, he prepares the way for twenty men, each of whom is perhaps not equal to him, but the twenty together are five times as great as he was. He distributes himself, and is buried and lives again in the tendencies which he has educated.

Every one that is working for men, patiently and

generously, no matter how humbly, is working for God. The fact that you are working for God brings all things to a level. The lowest thing is exalted when it is for God, and the highest thing, when it is for God, is not much higher than the lowest. The last shall be first, and the first shall be last.

* * *

We are not, as necessary as we think. The sun will come up to-morrow if you do die. The stars will shine if you are not here to see them. Summer will come if your plough lies still. The world is not made to turn on you as a pivot. You occupy a very small place. Your little will, and your little purposes, scarcely crease the great orb of affairs. And no man is so necessary that of stones God cannot raise up one to take his place. The work that you have in undivided hands, God scatters and divides up among hundreds.

* * *

Do not keep the alabaster boxes of your love and tenderness sealed up until your friends are dead. Fill their lives with sweetness. Speak approving, cheering words while their ears can hear them, and while their hearts can be thrilled by them. The things you mean to say when they are gone, say before they go. The flowers you mean to send for their coffins, send to brighten and sweeten their homes before they leave them. If my friends have alabaster boxes laid away, full of perfumes of sympathy and affection, which they intend to break over my dead body, I would rather they would bring them out in my weary hours, and open them, that I may be refreshed and cheered by them while I need them.

* * *

I would rather have a bare coffin without a flower, and funeral without a eulogy, than a life without the sweetness of love and sympathy. Let us learn to anoint our friends beforehand for their burial. Post-mortem kindness does not cheer the burdened spirit. Flowers on the coffin cast no fragrance backward over the weary days.

* * *

Whether or not you are as good as the next man depends upon who the next man is.

* * *

It is the amount of mentality which men put into their work that determines their place, their wages and their honor.

* * *

The great law, the real law which determines the value of the services of men and of the products they produce, is that of mind. The value of these things depends upon the kind and the quantity of the mind that is put into them. He that employs common mental power in his work takes common wages. He that employs superior powers of mind in his work takes higher wages. He who has talents that every body needs and stands pre-eminent, like some distinguished barrister at the bar, or like some wonderful artist at canvas, because he puts into his work more mind of better quality, than anybody else, gets the highest price for his labor.

The real law, the underlying principle is, that the value of men's work, and of the products of their work, is to be determined by the amount of mind and the quality of mind which enters into them.

* *
*

What if a man should go out with the theory that it was his province to bring wheat and rye and barley to one and the same scale, and that it was a corrupt market that gave a different price for each? What if he should act on the principle that all grains should be valued alike, not only, but that chaff should be reckoned in the same category? It would be about as sensible as the attempt in the great labor-market to lump men together, and equalize them, high and low, strong and weak, skilled and unskilled, and make them all alike, cutting down all natural processes of ranking.

A war between England and America would be like

murder in the family — unnatural — monstrous beyond words to depict. Now, then, if that be so, it is our duty to avoid all cause and occasion of offence. But remember — remember — remember — we are carrying out our dead. Our sons, brothers' sons, our sisters' children — they are in this great war of liberty and of principle. We are taxing all our energies; you are at peace, and if in the flounderings of this gigantic conflict we accidentally tread on your feet, are we or you to have most patience? When the widowed mother sits watching the shortening breath of her child, hovering between life and death — it may be that the rent has not been paid — it may be that her fuel has not yet been settled for; but what would you think of that landlord or of that provision dealer that would send a warrant of distress when the funeral was going out of the door, and arrest her when she was walking to the grave with her first-born son. Even a brute would say, "Wait — wait!" Yet it was in the hour of our mortal anguish, that when, by an unauthorized act, one of the captains of our navy seized a British ship for which our government instantly offered all reparation, that a British army was hurried to Canada.

I have felt from the first that I hold a higher allegiance than any I owe to man — to God, and to that truth which is God's ordinance in human affairs, and for the sake of that higher truth, I have loved my country, but I have loved truth more than my country.

I have heard the voice of my Master, saying, "If any man come unto me and hate not father and mother, and brother and sister, yea and his own life also, he is not worthy of me". When, therefore, the cause of truth and justice is put in the scale against my own country, I would disown country for the sake of truth; and when the cause of truth and justice is put in the scale against Great Britian, I would disown her rather than betray what I understood to be the truth. We are bound to establish liberty, regulated Christian liberty, as the law of the American Continent.

Slavery we always hated; the Southern men never. They were wrong. And in our conflicts with them we have felt as all men in conflict feel. We were jealous, and so were they. We were in the right cause; they in the wrong. We were right, or liberty is a delusion; they were wrong, or slavery is a blessing.

***

Now anybody that is a great poet does not have to pump. It is the nature in him that rules him, and he can't help himself. He does not need to send out to see what this man thinks of it. It is the necessity of expressing one's self that makes a man a poet. And a man that is an orator is simply a man that has something to say. It rules him, and rides him. He never runs panting along the dusty way of industry, trying to hunt for eloquence. Whoever does that never catches it.

And now the martyr is moving in triumphal march, mightier than when alive. The nation rises up at every stage of his coming. Cities and States are his pall-bearers, and the cannon beats the hours with solemn progression. Dead, dead, dead, he yet speaketh! Is Washington dead? Is Hamden dead? Is David dead? Is any man that ever was fit to live dead? Disenthralled of flesh, and risen in the unobstructed sphere where passion never comes, he begins his illimitable work. His life now is grafted upon the Infinite, and will be fruitful as no earthly life can be. Pass on, thou that hast overcome!

Join with us then, Britons. From you we learnt the doctrine of what a man was worth; from you we learned to detest all oppressions; from you we learnt that it was the noblest thing a man could do to die for a principle. And now, when we are set in that very course, and are giving our best blood for principle let the world understand that when America strikes for the liberty of the slave, and of the common people, Great Britian endorses her.

Let all the nations stand off! Sweep around the

ring, and stand off spectators, and now let these gigantic forms stand — Liberty and God — Slavery and the Devil — and no more put hand or foot into that ring until they have done battle unto the death.

* * *

Union is good if it is Union for justice and liberty; but if it is Union for slavery, then it is thrice accursed.

* * *

Self-contemplation has no power to do any good. We must look out of self if we want to grow, not in. A ship-master might as well look into the hold of his ship for the North Star, as a man into his own heart for guidance and encouragement. We learn faith and hope and courage, by looking up to Christ, not down into ourselves.

No man was ever yet made deep enough to satisfy himself. Forget that you live at all, in the absorbing sense that Christ liveth in you. Where the heart is fullest there is the most unconsciousness of itself.

INDEX.

Adversity	85-92
Advice	304-305
Aspiration	138-142
Atonement	42-48
Books	207-208
Beauty, Love of	304-306
Ballot, The	98-99
Brotherhood of Man	222-227
Bible, The	155-165
Christ, Divinity of	16-21
Christ, Personal	32-42
Consummation	175-179
Christianity	256-257
Capacity	236-237
Christian, The True	195-201
Compassion, God's	253-259
Contentment	234-236
Character	208-210
Creeds	73-76
Conceit	320
Cross Bearing	314-316
Cheerfulness	297-298
Conviction	296-297
Conversion	184-188
Conscience	281-283

INDEX.

Care, Anxious	179-184
Childhood	121-126
Children, Death of	119-121
Contemplation, Self	342
Death	92-94
Duty	50-53
Doubt	111-112
Emotion	227-229
Education	325-327
Exaltation of Spirit	782-783
Envying	312
Evolution	165-167
Eloquence	338-342
Enthusiasm	267-269
Experience	276-281
Election	295-296
Faith	48-50
Fear	53-54
Friendship	312-314
Feeling	215-218
Fiction	194-195
Future, The	83-85
Flowers	324-325
Faults	201-207
God	21-32
Gentleness	231-232
Grace	190-194
Generosity	100-110
Genius	112
Growth	142-152
Greatness, True	110-112
Gospel, The	239-241
Heroism	265-267
Happiness	232-234
Humor	221-222
Holiness	94-95
Home	320

Heaven	169-175
Harmony	317-319
Heart, The	320
Health	308-309
Hope	294-295
Inspiration	92-93
Ignorance	293-294
Influence, Divine	61-68
Illimitable, Work	335-336
Immortality	342-348
Intelligence	305-306
Invisible, The	328-332
Impulse	221-222
Imagination	210-211
Joy	229-231
Knowledge	290-293
Laws	257-261
Lying	306-308
Life	78-83
Lord's Supper, The	211-214
Liberality	100-101
Liberty	1-6
Labor, Value of	337-338
Love	6-16
Motherhood	184
Manhood, Christian	131-138
Morality	244-346
Meekness	99-100
Mourning	97-98
Motives	334-335
Mistakes	221
Marriage	298-299
Names	189-190
Nature	76-78
Opportunity	319-320
Ordinances	248-251
Prayer	101-109

Preaching	283-290
Patience	301-302
Peace	302-303
Probation	295-296
Profession of Religion	238-239
Providence, God's	241-244
Religion	54-61
Resurrection	320
Right, Vindication of	321-324
Regeneration	248-249
Revivals	246-248
Responsibility, Moral	263-264
Repentance	274-276
Retribution, Future	309-312
Sunday	188-189
Science	113-116
Solitude	167-169
Silence	167-169
Suffering	126-131
Selfishness	299-301
Soul-life	95-97
Sentiment	241
Success	214-215
Sin	269-274
Sympathy	336-337
Self-denial	218-221
Truth	68-73
Taste	321
Trouble	116-119
Trust	316-317
Teaching, Christ's	303-304
Tongue, The	264-265
Temptation	332-334
Wealth	152-155
Work	253-256
Waiting	261-263
Words	109-110

www.ingramcontent.com/pod-product-compliance
Lightning Source LLC
Chambersburg PA
CBHW020236240426
43672CB00006B/543